THE BEST BIKE RIDES IN THE SOUTH

**Alabama · Florida · Georgia
Mississippi · North Carolina
South Carolina · Tennessee · Virginia**

by

Elizabeth and Charles Skinner

Pequot
press

Old Saybrook, Connecticut

Library of Congress Cataloging-in-Publication Data

Skinner, Elizabeth, 1961-
  The best bike rides in the South / by Elizabeth and Charles Skinner. — 1st ed.
    p. cm.
  "A Voyager book."
  ISBN 1-56440-015-8
  1. Bicycle touring—Southern States—Guidebooks. 2. Southern States—Guidebooks. I. Skinner, Charlie, 1943- . II. Title.
GV1045.5.S67S55 1992
796.6′4′0975—dc20   92-13399
                                                                CIP

❖ This book is printed on recycled paper.
Manufactured in the United States of America
First Edition/First Printing

To our circle of family and friends

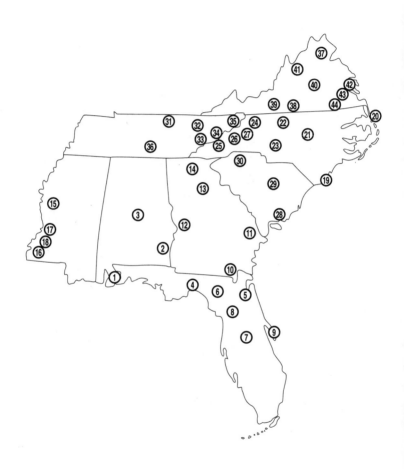

Contents

Introduction

The geography of the South is so varied that bicycling in the region can be fundamentally different from place to place. By mountain bike you can scream down rocky, forest-service roads in the Linville Gorge Wilderness Area on one weekend, only to roll through the saltwater marsh and sand dunes of the Outer Banks on the next. You can experience a sensory overload of tree greens and wild-flower pastels on mile-long descents along the Blue Ridge Parkway. You can pedal in a haze of summer heat to the drone of crickets and the groan of bullfrogs in the swampland of your choice.

Perhaps you prefer to embellish your bicycle tours with histori-cal significance and culinary delights. For you, the South offers tours of Virginia's wine country, complete with wine tastings and back-road rambling; inn-to-inn excursions where southern hospi-tality is paramount; tours to the historic southern cities of Savan-nah, Charleston, Williamsburg, and Jamestown; bicycle trails along converted railroad beds steeped in railroad lore; and rides for bird enthusiasts through natural habitats, such as the St. Marks Wildlife Refuge and the Okeefenokee Swamp.

The South offers year-round bicycling possibilities in each of the eight states covered here. Mild winters, with average temperatures in the seventies, have made Florida a popular training location for racers in the off-season. In fact, many of the rides featured along the Atlantic Coast and Florida are best explored in fall, winter, and spring. The southern states can be oppressively humid from May through September.

Much of the best bicycling in the South explores the rambling network of country back roads that wind through orange groves, pecan orchards, and horse pastures; through fields of tobacco, peaches, peanuts, and cotton.

Four distinctive parkways maintained by the National Park Ser-vice provide outstanding cycling conditions. The Natchez Trace Parkway in Tennessee and Mississippi, the Skyline Drive in Virginia, the Blue Ridge Parkway in Virginia and North Carolina, and the Colonial Parkway in the Williamsburg area combine scenic beauty with historic significance. Each of these parkways is highly recommended for weekend bicycle tours or more ambitious, extended tours.

Several southern bicycle clubs have created noteworthy annual events with colorful traditions and devoted followers. For sixteen years the Cross-Florida Ride, organized by the Spacecoast Freewheelers of Cocoa Beach, has been challenging cyclists to join the pace line for a 170-mile blur across the Sunshine State. TOSRV, sponsored by the Capital City Cyclists in Tallahassee, Florida, tours through rolling, red clay hills at the height of an azalea and dogwood blooming frenzy. BRAG, the Bicycle Ride Across Georgia, invites cyclists to spend a relaxing week touring the state. Tennessee has its BRAT, Virginia its Bike Virginia, South Carolina its Fun Ride of South Carolina, and Florida its Florida Classical Safari. The Spartanburg Freewheelers of South Carolina attract sixteen hundred bicyclists each May for their annual Assault on Mt. Mitchell, a 102-mile hill climb to the highest point east of the Mississippi.

A quick glance at *Bicycling* magazine's ride calendar, or the *Bicycle USA Almanac*'s state-by-state directory, attests to the popularity of bicycling in the South. *The Best Bike Rides in the South* highlights forty-four rides featuring a sampling of the outstanding scenery, historic intrigue, and challenging terrain this eight-state region has to offer. Whether you enjoy relaxed touring, blistering speed, or something in between, there are plenty of rides here for you.

Bicycling Southern Style

The Southern Climate

Hot, sweltering weather conditions are legendary in the South. Stereotypes on the heat alone have loaded innocuous objects with meaning . . . twirling parasols and rapidly fanning fans, chilled mint juleps, and tall, cool glasses of iced tea. Southern cyclists rarely have to remind themselves of the cycling adage "drink before you're thirsty." Natives are likely to know where every convenience store on every route is located and whether they stock Exceed, Gatorade, 10-K, Perrier, Tropicana Twisters, or Slurpees.

While ninety-degree heat can be miserable, four-season cycling makes the southern states prime cycling destinations in the winter months. Although arctic fronts do dip down as far as Florida, winter temperatures in the region average in the sixties and the seventies. Even Virginia and Tennessee experience mild winters on the whole. Mountainous areas are the most likely to experience severe winter weather. Coastal areas, from Virginia to Florida to Mississippi, are kept temperate by warm sea breezes from the Atlantic Ocean and the Gulf of Mexico.

Statistically, January is the coldest month in the South, while July and August are the hottest. Heat is certainly much more debilitating than most southern cold fronts ever could be. Keep in mind that the most oppressive areas for heat are inland where the land is cut off from any remnant of a sea breeze. Mississippi is infamous for its oppressive humidity. Jackson, Mississippi, has recorded humidity of 90 percent or higher during every month of the year. A famed front called the Bermuda high is notorious for stalling large heat masses over Georgia and the Carolinas.

Thunderstorms are another southern-summer trademark. The South, Florida especially, can be counted on for afternoon thunderstorms. It is wise to begin bike rides in the early morning hours from May through September to take advantage of cooler morning temperatures and to avoid afternoon thunderstorms entirely. If you do get caught in a summer storm, find shelter out of the elements and keep in mind that temperatures may drop suddenly ten or more degrees.

Hurricane season runs from June through November on the eastern seaboard. Be advised that travel plans may be seriously thwarted by tropical storms or possible hurricanes. Brewing storms are usually forecast well in advance, although not far enough to affect plans made months ahead of time.

The South is also known for swampy areas, especially in Florida, Georgia, South Carolina, Virginia, and Mississippi. Several rides, including the Okefenokee Swamp Cruise, the Mississippi Delta

Cruise, and the Emporia "Great Peanut" Challenge, pass through swampy areas. Beware of mosquitoes and other insect pests in high-moisture areas. Insect repellent should be carried as a basic supply item in the summer months.

Sunscreen should also be basic equipment for bike rides in the South. The Florida sun, especially, has been categorized as subtropical. Ultraviolet rays between the hours of ten o'clock and two o'clock can be particularly damaging. Good quality sunglasses will make your bike ride more pleasurable.

Clothing, Equipment, and Supplies

We have already mentioned sunscreen, sunglasses, and insect repellent as items of special value to cyclists in the southern states. Common sense and personal taste should dictate your choices in cycling apparel. Weather conditions are the single overriding factor when choosing bicycle clothing. Listen to the local forecast before venturing out, and choose your clothing accordingly. It is wise to carry a lightweight rain jacket for those afternoon thunderstorms so predictable in the summer months.

Helmets are the single-most-important piece of equipment you can wear as a cyclist. We strongly urge you to wear a helmet at all times when cycling. Head injuries are the leading cause of death in bicycling accidents. Take care to get a proper fit, and be sure to wear your helmet securely.

Staying on top of maintenance and repairs for your bicycle will prevent undue problems out on the road. Know how to fix a flat tire, and carry a few basic items on your bike at all times: an air pump (that attaches to the frame of your bicycle), spare tube, patch kit, chain breaker, spoke wrench, pliers, small adjustable wrench, allen wrenches, tire levers, and a multipurpose lubricant. You might also routinely carry a driver's license (or some other form of identification) and a few dollars in change for emergencies. These items should fit in a small bag mounted underneath the rear of your bicycle seat.

Please be sure to fill your water bottles before every ride. It is always critical for cyclists to drink plenty of liquids. Remember to drink *before* your body tells you it's thirsty. If you wait for thirst, it may be too late to rehydrate your system. Heat exhaustion and heat stroke can be real problems in the summer months. Drinking ample fluids will guard against problems.

Signs of heat exhaustion include faintness, rapid pulse, nausea, profuse sweating, cool skin, and collapse. Heat stroke is characterized by fever, hot and dry skin, and rapid pulse. We do not want to sound overly dramatic, but reactions to excessive heat do occur during intense exertion in high temperatures.

Bicycling Etiquette and Safety

According to Barbara Savage in *Miles From Nowhere,* Florida drivers treat cyclists worse than do drivers in any other state. Of south and central Florida she says, "The basic philosophy these drivers adhered to was simple enough: all roads are constructed solely for motorized vehicles . . . the overwhelming majority of [motorists] responded in one of three ways. They either rode behind us and honked for what seemed like an eternity before roaring by as close as possible; or they pulled alongside us and filled the air with raging obscenities; or they opted for the silent, direct approach and tried to hit us." In all fairness, this is an overstatement. Yet it does go far in illustrating the tension that can arise between bicyclists and motorists.

Try to be attuned to the prevailing attitudes of the residents in areas you bicycle through. Always ride single file and to the right side of the road. Obey all traffic laws. If you bicycle in a responsible manner, you can expect motorists to respect your right to share the road.

Most of the routes included in *The Best Bike Rides in the South* travel on roads with low traffic, but there is occasional congestion. Strive for a happy coexistence with motorists. And again, *wear a helmet at all times.*

Have Fun Out There!

The best way to ensure a good time bicycling is to know your capabilities as a rider. Know your body and its limits. Read the ride descriptions carefully, and choose routes that you can enjoy. The longer rides require a good solid training base. Think twice before cycling a route that is more than 20 miles longer than the distances you regularly cycle.

How to Use This Book

Choosing Between Touring, Racing, and Mountain Bikes

The Best Bike Rides in the South includes rides appropriate for touring, racing, and mountain bikes. A handful of the rides in the book follow off-road routes on unpaved surfaces. These rides are intended for mountain bikes. Each mountain-bike ride featured in the book is designated as such.

All rides not labeled as mountain-bike rides are suitable for touring or racing bikes. They travel down reasonably good to well-paved road surfaces. Mountain bikes are fine on paved surfaces, too. A few routes have short sections of rough pavement. These brief sections may determine whether you opt for your racing bike or your touring bike. The Roan Mountain Challenge is a perfect example of a road ride that includes a brief, 1-mile gravel stretch.

We presume that you have the luxury of choice. We hope you do. If you do not yet own a mountain bike, borrow a friend's (or rent one from a bike shop) and check out one of the mountain-bike routes. You may get hooked on off-road cycling.

Ride Categories

Each ride is rated according to level of difficulty. Every ride has been named either "ramble," "cruise," "challenge," or "classic" to correspond with the general bicycling categories of easy, moderate, intermediate, and difficult.

Rambles are leisurely rides ranging from 10 to 35 miles in length. While designed primarily for beginning cyclists, they can be enjoyed by cyclists of all abilities. Rambles are ideal for cyclists traveling quickly through an area. All rambles can be completed in a morning or afternoon. Expect primarily flat terrain, although a few rambles are in hilly or mountainous terrain.

Cruises cover distances between 35 and 50 miles over flat to hilly terrain. Cruises offer solid mileage to intermediate and advanced cyclists, while beginning riders can expect a fairly rigorous workout.

Challenges range between 50 and 75 miles. Rides in this category are not for beginners, although many challenges feature overnight touring options that spread the distance over two days. Keep heat and humidity in mind when selecting your distance. Extremely hot conditions can make a challenge seem more like a classic.

Classics are the toughest rides in the book. Plan to make these rides an all-day affair. Most classics exceed 75 miles in length, although some are a bit shorter. Classics require a confident assessment of individual cycling fitness. Classics will merit their difficult rating for a variety of reasons: strenuous climbs in hilly and mountainous terrain, long distances (in many cases, 100-mile "century" routes), or a combination of the two.

Read the description of each ride carefully before heading out. When traveling to a specific state or region, read up on all the rides featured in that area and consider overnight options. As we stated above, longer rides may be more enjoyable spread out over two days. There are so many excellent inns and campgrounds along routes with exciting points of interest that overnight touring is the preferred choice for rides like the Linville Gorge Classic, the Storming of Thunder Ridge Classic, and the Ocala Horse Country Challenge.

Always use caution when undertaking distances more than twice as long as any rides you have cycled before. If you are inexperienced at cycling in mountainous terrain, choose a conservative distance. Mountainous terrain truly magnifies the difficulty of certain rides, particularly in Great Smoky Mountains National Park and the Blue Ridge Mountains.

Acknowledgments

The Best Bike Rides in the South represents the energy and enthusiasm of individual bike club members all over the southeast who stepped forward with bike rides they enjoy. Nearly every ride in this book was pioneered by an individual, group, or organization other than ourselves. As you read each ride, you will meet the cyclists who introduced us to the forty-four rides represented here.

We would like to give a special thanks to Jeanne Hargrave of the North Florida Bicycle Club; she helped research several Florida rides on one very rainy weekend. Thanks also to Joe Cross, who introduced us to the riches of the Big South Fork area, and Bobbie Wren, founder and gracious host of the Great Peanut Ride in Emporia, Virginia.

A final thanks goes to the League of American Wheelmen for the outstanding resources it provides to touring cyclists nationwide.

Road Abbreviations

The following abbreviations have been used to designate road names throughout the book:

AL-, GA-, etc.	Primary state routes
CR-	County Road
Hwy.	Highway
I–	Interstate Highway
Rte.	Route
SR-	State Road
US-	United States Highway

Alabama

BIRMINGHAM •

③

• MONTGOMERY

②

MOBILE •

①

Alabama

1

Gulf Coast Challenge

Gulf State Park Resort—Magnolia Springs
Point Clear—Fairhope—Point Clear
Magnolia Springs—Gulf State Park Resort

Of all the states along the Gulf of Mexico, Alabama enjoys the briefest segment of coastline. Although scant in mileage, this sugary white section of beachfront has been prominent throughout the history of the region. From the prehistoric activity of Creek, Choctaw, Chickasaw, and Cherokee Indians to busy commerce as an exporter of cotton, the Mobile Bay area has been central to the growth of the region.

The American Lung Association of Alabama hosts its Breath of Life Bike Trek each September, introducing bicyclists to exciting areas of Alabama. The Gulf Coast Bike Trek has been a popular tour. Laura Vann, director of public relations for the American Lung Association of Alabama (and an avid cyclist herself), raves about the sparkling coastline, gently rolling farmland, and bayside towns of Baldwin County.

Beginning at the Gulf State Park Resort in Gulf Shores, Alabama, the Gulf Coast Challenge heads north from the Gulf of Mexico inland past live oak, magnolia, and pecan trees into a coastal plain of lush farmland. From the town of Magnolia Springs, the route heads west crossing over the Weeks Bay Bridge past the Weeks Bay National Estuarine Reserve. Highway 98 hugs the eastern shore of Mobile Bay past residential waterfront property with glimpses of the bay. Along the way you will ride through the village of Point Clear, past Marriott's Grand Hotel, and on to the fishing village of Fairhope. A stunning ride into Fairhope Municipal Pier and Park affords glimmering views of Mobile Bay.

At mile 34, Fairhope Public Pier marks the halfway point and turnaround for the tour. This picturesque bayside village makes an ideal break point. Stroll along the pier, then cruise through town in search of the perfect café. Fairhope supports a thriving community of painters, sculptors, woodworkers, and other artists. Craft lovers may be tempted to spend the afternoon browsing through downtown shops, or better yet, plan on catching the annual Eastern Shore Arts and Crafts Festival in the spring. From Fairhope the course makes an inland loop back to Magnolia Springs and south to Gulf State Park.

The Gulf Coast Challenge offers several options for touring cyclists. A wide variety of accommodations provides for every taste. The area virtually demands an overnight stay somewhere along the route. You might set up a base camp at Gulf State Park and cycle the full loop in a day. For a bit more indulgence, why not pamper yourself with a stay at one of the beachfront resorts, either Marriott's Grand Hotel or the Gulf State Park Resort. Both resorts feature golf, swimming, and beachcombing sure to please noncyclists among family and friends.

Laura Vann emphasizes that the coastal highways are well traveled in the summer months. Traffic on Highway 59 leading out of Gulf Shores can be moderately heavy from midmorning to late afternoon. And while very scenic, traffic on Highway 98 moves at a brisk pace, so caution is encouraged. Spring and fall may be the best seasons for cycling in the Gulf Coast Challenge, as crowds are considerably diminished and humidity is much lower.

The Basics

Start: The ride begins at the Gulf State Park Resort off AL-135 in Gulf Shores. Park at the Gulf State Park Resort.
Length: 70.5 miles.

Terrain: Flat to rolling.
Food: Stores and restaurants are available in Gulf Shores, Magnolia Springs, Point Clear, and Fairhope.
For more information: American Lung Association of Alabama, 900 S. 18th St., P.O. Box 55209, Birmingham, AL 35255; (205) 933–8821.

Miles & Directions

- 0.0 Left leaving Gulf State Park Resort.
- 0.1 Right onto AL-135 North into park.
- 2.2 Left onto AL-180 West.
- 2.6 Right onto AL-59 North.
- 9.0 Left onto CR-12 (Baldwin Pools and Spas).
- 14.0 Right onto CR-49 North (second stop sign).
- 16.3 Left onto Hwy. 98 West.
- 20.7 Weeks Bay Bridge.
- 24.7 Straight onto Alt. Hwy. 98 West to Point Clear.
- 30.9 Grand Hotel.
- 34.0 Left at stop sign down to Fairhope Public Pier.
- 34.2 Right back on same route (Alt. Hwy. 98) all the way past Point Clear.
- 38.6 Left on CR-32.
- 40.5 Cross over 98. **Caution: Dangerous intersection.**
- 46.1 Right on CR-9 (four-way stop) at Aney's Texaco Station.
- 47.3 Left on AL-28 East (follow Baldwin County Animal Shelter signs).
- 48.7 Right on CR-49 South (be on the lookout, not well marked).
- 52.7 Cross 98 East Hwy.
- 53.2 Left at stop sign continuing on CR-49 South.
- 54.0 Left onto CR-26.
- 57.0 Right onto CR-65 South (four-way stop).
- 61.0 Left onto CR-10 (second four-way stop).
- 63.0 Right onto AL-59 South.
- 69.0 Left onto 182 East (at dead end of AL-59).
- 70.5 End at Gulf State Park Resort.

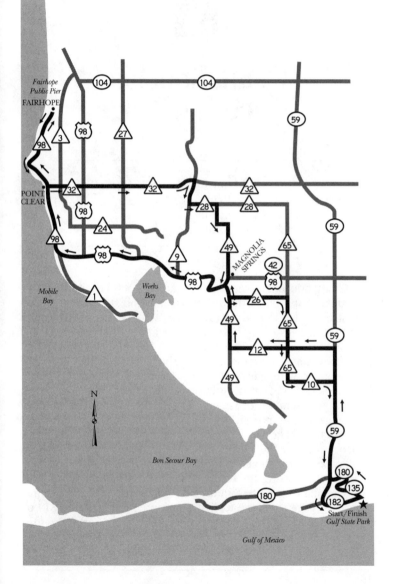

2

Chattahoochee Trace Challenge

White Oak Creek Park—Fort Gaines
Walter F. George Lock and Dam—Georgetown
Eufaula—White Oak Creek Park

The Chattahoochee River forms a natural boundary between the Wiregrass region of southeastern Alabama and the southwest corner of Georgia. The American Lung Association of Alabama's Breath of Life Bike Trek has twice cycled over the high bluffs that overlook the Chattahoochee River. The Chattahoochee River Challenge makes a 51-mile loop around the Chattahoochee River and Lake Eufaula, with side trips to Fort Gaines, the Walter F. George Lock and Dam, and the historic city of Eufaula.

Saving exploration of Eufaula for last, the Chattahoochee River Challenge heads out from White Oak Creek Park along 45,000-acre Lake Eufaula. Lake Eufaula was created by damming the Chattahoochee River at the Walter F. George Lock and Dam. Numerous small parks dot the shoreline, offering fine views of the lake and river.

Just after crossing the calm waters of the Chattahoochee River into Georgia, the route approaches Fort Gaines. The Fort Gaines Frontier Village features a replica of a frontier fort built in 1814 on a bluff overlooking the Chattahoochee River. From Fort Gaines the route heads 2 miles north to the East Bank area. Stop here for a tour of the second-highest lock lift in the United States.

The second half of the Chattahoochee River Challenge hugs the Georgia bank of the Chattahoochee and Lake Eufaula. It's 20 miles to Eufaula, so relax and enjoy the rolling-to-hilly terrain on sparsely traveled Georgia Highway 39.

The Old Jailhouse in Eufaula marks mile 41 on this tour. If you started your ride early, you've allowed plenty of time for tooling around Eufaula. Named for an area tribe of the Creek Confederacy, Eufaula features several Greek revival and neoclassical homes and buildings constructed in the mid-1800s when Eufaula served as a major embarkment for cotton. The Shorter Mansion (1884), the Sheppard Cottage (1837), and the Hart-Milton House (1843) are all open for tours. Eufaula hosts an annual "Eufaula Pilgrimage" tour of homes in early April.

Cotton most definitely fueled the economy up through the Civil War. The Chattahoochee River supported more than 125 steamboats traveling from Columbus, Georgia, to the Apalachicola Bay in the three decades leading up to the war. When you bicycle the surrounding countryside, you will notice that soybean and peanuts have replaced cotton as major crops in the region. Pine forests also predominate in the area, supporting a thriving lumber industry.

There are several options for cycling the Chattahoochee River Challenge. Two excellent state parks offer a variety of recreational activities for visitors in the area. The George T. Bagby State Park is located within cycling distance of the route off GA-39 4 miles north of Fort Gaines. While not directly on the route, Lakepoint Resort State Park, north of Eufaula, offers swimming and boating on Lake Eufaula.

Eufaula has several hotels and St. Mary's Bed and Breakfast for those who prefer indoor accommodations. Lodges at Lakepoint Resort State Park and George T. Bagby State Park offer gracious lakefront facilities.

Explore the Chattahoochee Trace by bike and by foot for a close-up look at the history of Native Americans and settlers along the banks of the Chattahoochee River.

The Basics

Start: The ride begins at White Oak Creek Park south of Eufaula on US-431.

Length: 51.0 miles.

Terrain: Rolling to hilly.

Food: Stores and restaurants are available in Fort Gaines at 17 miles, Georgetown at about 40 miles, and Eufaula at 42 miles.

For more information: American Lung Association of Alabama, 900 S. 18th St., P.O. Box 55209, Birmingham, AL 35255; (205) 933–8821.

Miles & Directions

- 0.0 White Oak Creek Park.
- 0.2 Right onto AL-95.
- 2.2 Left onto CR-97 (Old River Rd.).
- 6.3 Veer left on CR-97.
- 13.5 Left at stop sign/dead end. After this left turn, continue straight, do not turn right on CR-97.
- 14.0 Left to Walter F. George Lock and Dam. Follow the dam road.
- 15.3 Veer right at dam, and continue on road below the dam area.
- 16.6 Left at stop sign/dead end onto Buddy Crawford Rd. Proceed straight across bridge over the Chattahoochee River.
- 17.1 Left onto Jackson St. (leading to Frontier Village).
- 17.2 Left on Carroll St.
- 17.3 Frontier Village. Leaving Frontier Village, follow Bluff St.
- 17.4 Right onto Jefferson St. (at tennis courts).
- 17.7 Left onto Hancock St. (becomes Eufaula Rd.) and follow GA-39 North.
- 19.5 Entrance to east side of Walter F. George Lock and Dam (access to lock area from this side).
- 19.8 East Bank Area (rest rooms).
- 35.4 Triangular Crossroads (no rest rooms).

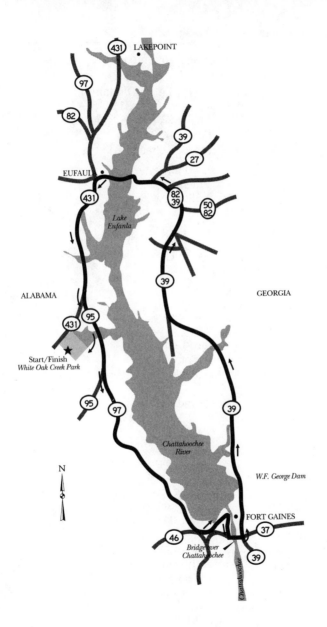

- 36.8 Left onto West US-82/GA-39 North to Georgetown.
- 41.4 Cross state line on bridge (US-82) to Eufaula.
- 41.6 Right onto Riverside Dr. to Old Jailhouse.
- 42.2 Left onto Eufaula Ave. (US-431).
- 47.7 Four-lane road narrows to two-lane.
- 48.9 Left onto AL-95 South.
- 50.8 Right into White Oak Creek Park.
- 51.0 Parking lot.

3

Columbiana Cruise

Chelsea—Columbiana—Chelsea

Cahaba Cycles—of Cahaba Heights, south of Birmingham—recommends the Columbiana Cruise for cyclists hoping to beat the congestion of the city. Beginning in the hamlet of Chelsea, Alabama, the loop explores the charming back roads of Shelby County southeast of Birmingham.

You'll ride along winding country roads past cemeteries, churches, and farmhouses. Featuring nothing spectacular to see or do, the Columbiana Cruise is the pleasant sort of bike ride that every bicyclist has in his or her basic repertoire.

Chelsea is a crossroads with a video store, a gas pump, and a country store. Find a place to park here, and you're off. In a matter of minutes you make a left turn onto Pumpkin Swamp Road, a rambling, canopied back road. Pumpkin Swamp takes you past pastures and cornfields. A one-lane wooden bridge crosses over Yellowleaf Creek.

From the creek to Columbiana, you'll pass Union Church, Ray Cemetery, and Blue Springs Church. On the way back from Columbiana, you pass by Lesters Chapel Church. These simple, white-clapboard churches—stalwart houses of faith and refuge—are the major landmarks of the area.

Columbiana is a pleasant town. Cahaba Cycles recommends stopping for lunch at House of Plenty on Business Route AL-25 for "real gut-busting traditional Southern fare." Columbiana is worth exploring for its small-town storefronts of hardware and five-and-dime stores. The Shelby County Courthouse draws the eye with its gleaming copper domes. The original courthouse, designed in classical Jeffersonian style, stands off on the left end of downtown. If you pass through Columbiana Monday through Friday between 8:30 A.M. and 4:00 P.M., be sure to step inside the Archives and Museum housed in the old courthouse.

From Columbiana, it's 12 miles back to Chelsea on more rambling back roads. The Columbiana Cruise is the perfect Sunday morning excursion. Pick a fresh spring day, or a crisp fall one, for the best cycling conditions.

If you're passing through Birmingham, this loop will work out all of your traveling aches and stiffness. Nearby Oak Mountain State Park has a pleasant campground for those looking for a weekend getaway. The park has extensive facilities featuring a golf course, swimming and fishing lake, and swimming pool.

The Basics

Start: To get to Chelsea from I–65 South, take AL-119 North 8.6 miles. Turn right on AL-280 East and go 6 miles. Turn right onto CR-47 South. Parking in Chelsea.

Length: 32.7 miles.

Terrain: Rolling hills to flat.

Food: There are country stores (if they're open) at 16.1 and 17.1 miles. Columbiana has several fast-food restaurants in addition to the illustrious House of Plenty at 19.8 miles.

For more information: Cahaba Cycles, 3120 Cahaba Heights Village, Birmingham, AL 35243.

Miles & Directions

- 0.0 From Chelsea head south on CR-47 South.
- 3.0 Turn left following CR-49 South.
- 3.2 Left onto CR-32 East (Pumpkin Swamp Rd.).
- 4.7 Wooden bridge crosses Yellowleaf Creek. Use caution.

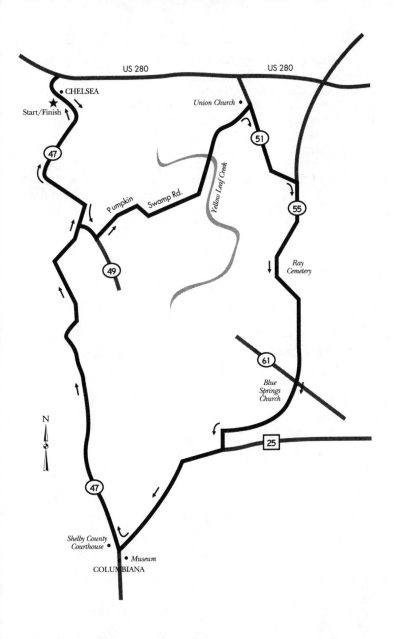

- 7.6 Right onto CR-51.
- 8.9 Right onto CR-55 South.
- 11.0 Ray Cemetery.
- 13.8 Junction CR-55 and CR-61. Stay on CR-55 South.
- 13.9 Blue Springs Church on the right.
- 16.0 Right onto AL-25 South.
- 19.0 Left following AL-25 East (Business).
- 20.3 Downtown Columbiana. The copper-domed Shelby County Courthouse is to the right. The original courthouse and museum is 0.1 mile to the left. To continue on route, turn right onto CR-47 North.
- 29.6 Go straight on CR-47 North.
- 32.7 You're back in Chelsea.

Florida

Florida

4

St. Marks Cruise

Tallahassee—St. Marks—Newport
St. Marks Wildlife Refuge

This cruise begins on St. Marks Trail, a 10-foot-wide, paved recreation trail (converted from an old railroad bed) that runs 16.2 miles to the town of St. Marks. Open to bicyclists, hikers, and horsemen and women, the trail follows the route of the Tallahassee-to-St. Marks Railroad, the first railroad in Florida to receive a federal land grant. Sandy Madsen, the sole ranger for the Tallahassee–St. Marks Historic Railroad State Trail, beams with pride in her job of overseeing the maintenance of the trail. Remarkably free of debris, the trail is swept clean by blowers once a week. According to the ranger's statistics, more than 4,500 visitors use the trail each month. Sandy says the best time to cycle the trail is by the light of a full moon.

From St. Marks, cyclists can either head back to Tallahassee or venture beyond the trail to the St. Marks National Wildlife Refuge and the St. Marks Lighthouse, which was constructed in 1831. The refuge is a nesting place for ninety-eight species of birds, more than 300 species of birds have been sighted there. During the 10-mile ride through the refuge to the lighthouse, you may easily sight osprey, the southern bald eagle, and species of pelican and egret.

As you approach St. Marks Lighthouse, water shimmers in a vast panorama, and a gentle breeze blows off the Gulf of Mexico. Throughout the ride this breeze gradually intensifies as you near the Apalachee Bay. Fortunately, this slight head wind becomes an energizing tail wind for the travel back to Tallahassee.

Whether your destination is St. Marks or the refuge, allow your-self time to explore. While the St. Marks Trail can be cycled in a few hours, the trip to the refuge and lighthouse deserves the better part of a day. Stop inside the refuge visitors center to view wildlife dis-plays and chat with an interpretive ranger. The center asks for a minimal (voluntary) fee. Once in the refuge, take the time to roll your bike off onto the many hiking trails and dikes. If you stand or sit still long enough, you will experience the refuge on a deeper level. You'll see mullet break the water's surface in a silver slice. You could get an up-close, personal view of a gator. You might even lose yourself in the prehistoric timelessness of the place.

The Basics

Start: From the state capitol building in Tallahassee, take Monroe St., which merges into Woodville Hwy. (Hwy. 363) south to the outskirts of the city. The parking lot for the Tallahassee–St. Marks Historic Railroad State Trail is on your right.

Length: 32.4 or 51.8 miles.

Terrain: Flat with a slight head wind off the gulf.

Food: Home of the "topless oyster," Posey's Oyster Bar in St. Marks at mile 16.2 may be reason enough to do this tour. The town of Newport, between St. Marks and the lighthouse, has a small store. Drinking water is available at the visitors center in St. Marks Na-tional Wildlife Refuge.

Miles & Directions

- 0.0 The St. Marks Trail heads straight out from the parking lot. If you are unfamiliar with negotiating a bike path, use caution when approaching oncoming traffic on the 8-foot-wide path. Residential dirt and paved roads intersecting the trail are well marked.

- 13.2 The St. Marks Trail intersects Hwy. 98. Here you may either cross the intersection and continue on the trail to St. Marks, or

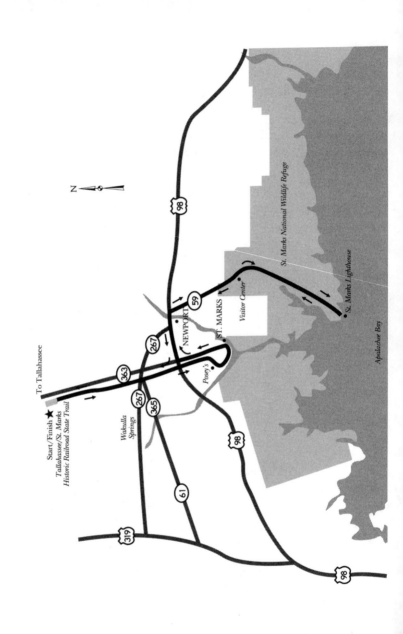

turn left onto Hwy. 98 and go 2.7 miles past the town of New-port, over the St. Marks River to the entrance of the St. Marks National Wildlife Refuge. Although Hwy. 98 is two-lane, it is amply wide for a car and a bike.

To complete the St. Marks Trail, cross Hwy. 98, and continue 3 miles to the town of St. Marks. Simply follow the trail back to Tallahassee for a total of 32.4 miles.

- 15.9 Turn right at the entrance to the St. Marks National Wild-life Refuge. The road into the refuge is C-59. This road is paved and traveled primarily by visitors to the lighthouse.
- 25.9 The road ends at the St. Marks Lighthouse. Simply retrace your route back to your starting point.
- 38.6 Back now to where the St. Marks Trail and Hwy. 98 inter-sect, you may want to cycle the 3 additional miles to Posey's Oyster Bar.

5

St. Johns River Challenge

Jacksonville—Bakersville
Molasses Junction—Spuds—Hastings
Riverdale—Tocoi—Picolata—Orangedale
Remington Forest—Switzerland—Julington Creek

One of the most remarkable images we carry with us of Jacksonville was formed when a solitary manatee surfaced one day as we were walking downtown along the St. Johns River. We marveled at the odds of sighting such a creature amid the speedboats, yachts, and watertaxis churning up the choppy waters. Northeast Florida is dominated by the St. Johns River, a broad river playground and the only major river in the United States whose current runs northward. In Duval County alone, six massive bridges transport an ever-increasing population back and forth from shore to shore. This population explosion presents danger and difficulty for cyclists.

The good news is that if you venture a bit beyond Duval County, the pace slows down considerably and excellent cycling can be experienced. The St. Johns River Challenge features five loops developed by the North Florida Bicycle Club for its "Endless Summer Watermelon Century Ride." With 35-, 50-, 65-, and 100-mile loops, there are options for all levels of ability. The longer loops offer the most history and beauty as they parallel the St. Johns River on the William Bartram Scenic Highway.

Between 1773 and 1777, the naturalist William Bartram explored the east coast of Florida interacting with the Creek and Semi-

---

nole Indians. He studied and catalogued plant life throughout the area this ride explores in what is now St. Johns County. Anyone interested in Florida's unique ecosystems will find William Bartram's writings fascinating.

Your bicycle should slow you down enough to focus upon the things that remain the same after 200 years, the water hyacinths floating on the broad St. Johns; the massive, insect hum of mosquitoes, gnats, dragonflies, and crickets; the live oak canopies dangling Spanish moss; the wide, blue sky that carries on a life of its own full of fat, purposeful clouds. Imagine how different Florida would be if you stripped away it's man-made gleam and glitter? It would be swampy and elemental: the real, natural Florida few people take the time to experience.

The Basics

Start: The Allen V. Nease High School parking lot off US-1 south of Jacksonville.
Length: 37.2, 51.6, 64.3, and 103.4 miles.
Terrain: Flat.
Food: There are plenty of country stores in the hamlets along the route. Check out Buddy Boy's Kountry Korner at the intersection of SR-13 and Joe Ashton Rd.
Special conditions: Beware extreme heat and humidity in the summer months. Bring plenty of water (and sunscreen) if you decide to tough it out. This ride would be most enjoyable September through April. Mosquitoes can be a problem, so consider bringing along the insect repellent.
For more information: North Florida Bicycle Club, P.O. Box 14294, Jacksonville, FL 32238; (904) 387–9858.

Miles & Directions

For the 37.2-mile option—
- 0.0 Right onto Old Dixie Hwy. North.

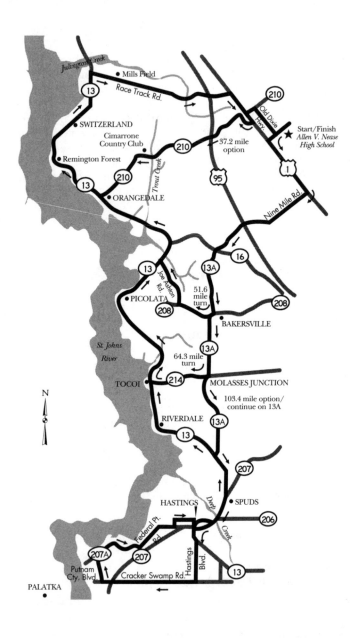

- ■ 1.5 Left onto SR-210 (Palm Valley Rd.).
- ■ 1.6 Left onto US-1 (Phillips Hwy.).
- ■ 2.3 Right onto SR-210.
- ■ 5.7 Cross I-95.
- ■ 14.1 Right onto SR-13. You are in Orangedale.
- ■ 18.1 Remington Forest.
- ■ 25.1 Right onto Race Track Rd.
- ■ 26.5 Mills Field Park (rest rooms).
- ■ 34.2 Right onto US-1 (Phillips Hwy.).
- ■ 37.2 Left onto Ray Rd. to Nease High School.

For the 51.6-mile option—

- ■ 0.0 Left onto US-1 South (Phillips Hwy.).
- ■ 5.1 Right onto Nine Mile Rd.
- ■ 12.1 Cross Hwy. 16, continue on SR-13A/Pacetti Rd.
- ■ 16.4 Right onto SR-208.
- ■ 18.8 Right onto Joe Ashton Rd.
- ■ 21.9 Right onto SR-13. Orangedale.
- ■ 32.5 Remington Forest.
- ■ 39.5 Right onto Race Track Rd.
- ■ 40.9 Mills Field Park (rest rooms).
- ■ 48.6 Right onto US-1 (Phillips Hwy.).
- ■ 51.6 Left onto Ray Rd. to Nease High School.

For the 64.3-mile option—

- ■ 0.0 Left onto US-1 South (Phillips Hwy.).
- ■ 5.1 Right onto Nine Mile Rd.
- ■ 12.1 Cross Hwy. 16, continue on SR-13A (Pacetti Rd.).
- ■ 16.4 Right on SR-208.
- ■ 16.7 Left onto SR-13A.
- ■ 20.4 Right onto SR-214. Molasses Junction.
- ■ 24.2 Right on SR-13.
- ■ 34.6 Orangedale.
- ■ 45.2 Remington Forest.
- ■ 52.2 Right onto Race Track Rd.

- 53.6 Mills Field Park (rest rooms).
- 61.3 Right onto US-1 (Phillips Hwy.).
- 64.3 Left onto Ray Rd. to Nease High School.

For the 103.4-mile option—

- 0.0 Left onto US-1 South (Phillips Hwy.).
- 5.1 Right onto Nine Mile Rd.
- 12.1 Cross Hwy. 16, continue on SR-13A (Pacetti Rd.).
- 16.4 Right on SR-208.
- 16.7 Left onto SR-13A.
- 20.4 Right onto SR-214. Molasses Junction.
- 20.7 Left onto SR-13A.
- 26.1 Left onto SR-13.
- 28.8 Right onto SR-207. **Caution: heavy traffic.**
- 29.9 Cross SR-206.
- 31.9 Left onto SR-13 (Main St.) at traffic light in downtown Hastings.
- 32.8 Right onto Old Hastings Blvd.
- 35.3 Right onto Cracker Swamp Rd. (rough pavement).
- 41.2 Right onto Putnam County Blvd. (railroad tracks).
- 42.9 Right at T onto CR-207A.
- 45.7 Left onto Federal Point Rd.
- 47.5 Right after small bridge, onto Old Hastings Blvd.
- 48.4 Left onto County Line Rd.
- 49.3 Right at T onto Federal Point Rd. (unmarked).
- 50.0 Right onto Main St. (in Hastings again).
- 51.5 Left onto SR-207. **Caution: heavy traffic.**
- 52.1 Cross SR-206.
- 53.2 Left onto SR-13.
- 61.7 Riverdale Park (rest rooms and telephone).
- 80.3 Orangedale.
- 84.3 Remington Forest.
- 91.3 Right onto Race Track Rd.
- 92.7 Mills Field Park (rest rooms).
- 100.4 Right onto US-1 (Phillips Hwy.).
- 103.4 Left onto Ray Rd. to Nease High School.

6

Suwannee River Classic

White Springs—Wellborn—Ichetucknee Springs
Falling Creek Falls—White Springs

For North Florida natives, the Suwannee River and Ichetucknee Springs conjure ready images of colorful history and gleeful childhood memories. Surely every child has spent a lazy summer day tubing down the brisk waters of Ichetucknee Springs, whiling away the time spotting turtles and ignoring thoughts of water moccasins and other exotic creatures. And no kid could escape Florida history lessons without the ability to recognize Stephen Foster's opening bars, "Way down upon the Suwannee River . . ."

It may be a revelation, for many visitors and natives alike, to discover this refreshingly underpopulated region of Florida with its network of scenic back roads. Lys Burden, tour director of Suwannee Bicycle Tours, has been busy exploring the riches of North Florida for her monthly "Suwannee Century Series" rides, all of which begin where our tour takes off at the headquarters of Suwannee Bicycle Tours in White Springs. The Suwannee River Challenge route is one of several tours conducted by SBT, which is a nonprofit, American Youth Hostels–affiliated bicycle touring company.

White Springs is a sleepy Florida town made notable by the Suwannee River, which runs through its middle, and by the Stephen Foster State Folk Culture Center. While Stephen Foster wrote "Old Folks at Home" without ever having seen the Suwannee River, the Culture Center will set the tone for your bicycle tour if you visit its exhibits before venturing out to explore the area. The

Culture Center sheds light on such phenomena as the "Florida Cracker," shape note singing, and the influence in Florida of immigrant cultures as diverse as Cuban, Czechoslovakian, and Scottish.

Although the Suwannee River winds throughout the area of this tour, you will only catch brief glimpses of it upon crossing bridges along your route. Before you leave the park, take time to cycle to the springhouse, or the boat landing, to study the river's dark, brooding waters, which flow south from their headwaters at the Okefenokee Swamp in Georgia. When the Suwannee is near flood levels, live oak trees will bow in wide arcs to meet the swiftly flowing river, leaving no clear delineation of where water ends and land begins.

With a few legends, a melody or two, and a vision of the Suwannee coloring your perceptions, you can pedal toward Ichetucknee Springs with your imagination racing ahead. We headed out to explore this route with Jeanne Hargrave, a member of the North Florida Bicycle Club. The landscape is predominantly agricultural with dairy and horse farms along the way. The most arresting view may be of the isolated Live Oaks sprawling in fields of bright green grass; the least engaging landscape is surely the inevitable slash pine forest with row upon row of tall, spindly pine.

The town of Wellborn is pleasant with its antique shops, restored homes, and historic churches. Fort White and O'Leno State Park are also worth exploring. On the back side of the tour, you may want to secure your bike and venture off the road on foot in search of Falling Creek Falls, a 12-foot waterfall that tumbles from a black-water creek. Before mounting your bike for the final miles back to White Springs, take time to appreciate Falling Creek Church, built out of heart pine more than a hundred years ago.

You have two options: the 98.2-mile century tour recommended by Suwannee Bicycle Tours or abbreviated routes going out and back from White Springs to Ichetucknee Springs State Park or O'Leno State Park. If you opt for the full loop, you might try camping at Ichetucknee Springs, allowing enough leisure time to cool off in the bracing waters of the springs. Ichetucknee Springs is sparkling clear in comparison to the Suwannee, with nine natural springs pumping 233 million gallons of water daily into the Ichetucknee River.

By exploring this tour, you will gain an appreciation for what the Florida State Parks mean by their slogan, "The Real Florida." If you're eager for more, sign up for one of Lys Burden's many tours of this bicycle-friendly area.

The Basics

Start: White Springs, Fla. From I–75 or I–10, take the White Springs exit. Suwannee Bicycle Association Headquarters is in "downtown" White Springs on Bridge St. (just around the bend on Hwy. 41 from the Stephen Foster Folk Culture Center).
Length: 98.2 miles.
Terrain: Flat to rolling.
Food: Convenience stores are located in Wellborn at 14.1 miles, at Ichetucknee Springs (37.0 miles), Ft. White (42.9 miles), the US-441 intersection, and White Springs.
Special conditions: Expect speed bumps at many intersections on roads along the route.
For more information: Suwannee Bicycle Tours, P.O. Box 247, White Springs, FL 32096. Florida Department of Natural Resources, Division of Recreation and Parks, Marjory Stoneman Douglas Building, 3900 Commonwealth Blvd., Tallahassee, FL 32399.

Miles & Directions

- 0.0 From the Suwannee Bicycle Association Headquarters, go west on SR-136.
- 0.2 Bridge over Suwannee River, enter Columbia County.
- 2.3 Enter Suwannee County.
- 3.1 I–75 overpass.
- 7.1 Left onto Hogan Rd.; no sign (Mt. Olive Baptist Church sign).
- 9.3 I–10 overpass.
- 13.5 Right onto CR-137.
- 14.1 Entering Wellborn.

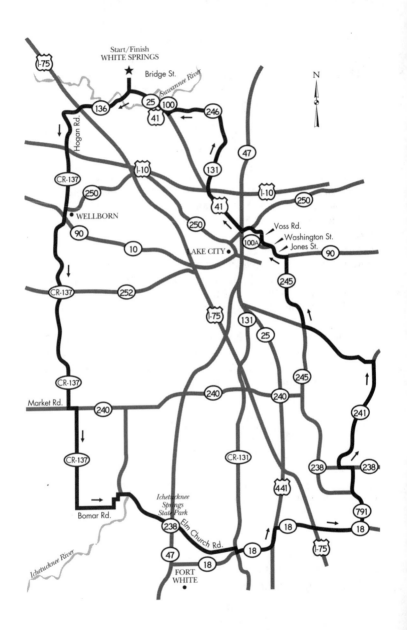

- 14.2 Cross SR-250 (old US-90) at flashing light. Use caution on speed bumps.
- 14.7 Cross US-90. More speed bumps.
- 19.3 Cross CR-252.
- 26.6 Left at T-intersection, CR-137 and SR-240.
- 27.1 Right onto CR-137.
- 28.3 Cross SR-247. More speed bumps.
- 33.1 Left onto Bomar Rd., just after billboard-sized BOMAR FARMS sign. Also sign for Ichetucknee Springs north entrance, 4.1 miles.
- 37.2 North entrance to Ichetucknee Springs State Park Rd. becomes CR-238 east of park entrance, entering Columbia County.
- 40.9 Cross SR-47, and road becomes Elm Church Rd.

For a 2-mile side trip into Fort White—

- 40.9 Right onto SR-47.
- 43.0 Left onto US-27 (flashing light) in Fort White.
- 43.3 Left onto CR-18 (signs for O'Leno State Park and Worthington Springs).
- 47.4 Cross CR-131.
- 49.7 Left onto US-441. Return to instructions at 47.7 miles below.
- 45.4 Right onto CR-131 (confusing 5-way intersection).
- 45.4 Left onto CR-18.
- 47.7 Left onto US-441. A right turn here takes you to O'Leno State Park, only 1.2 miles south, where there are miles of off-road opportunities.
- 48.8 Right onto CR-18.
- 51.0 I–75 overpass.
- 53.4 Enter Union County (apparently this county has no road signs).
- 54.2 Left onto CR-791 (Smith Rd.)—unmarked.
- 57.9 Left onto CR-238; no sign at this T-intersection.
- 58.7 Right onto CR-241.
- 65.1 Enter Columbia County.
- 65.9 Left onto CR-252; no sign.
- 70.8 Right onto CR-245; no sign, flashing light.

- 75.0 Cross SR-100.
- 75.5 Left onto US-90.
- 75.7 Right onto Jones St.
- 75.9 Left onto Washington St.
- 76.5 Right onto CR-100A.
- 77.5 Right onto Voss Rd.
- 79.0 Left onto CR-250.
- 79.5 Cross US-441 at traffic light; road becomes CR-25A.
- 82.6 Right onto US-41; use caution at I–10 interchange.
- 83.0 Right onto CR-131.
- 84.1 Bridge over Falling Creek. There is a trail on the north side of the bridge to Falling Creek Falls in the woods on the right.
- 84.2 Falling Creek Church is on the left.
- 87.9 Left onto CR-246.
- 91.1 Right onto US-41. Caution: US-41 has high-speed traffic.
- 92.1 Right onto Suwannee Valley Rd.
- 95.5 Right onto White Springs Rd.
- 97.8 Right onto SR-136.
- 98.2 Cross US-41; SR-136 becomes Bridge St. End at SBA/SBT headquarters on the right.

7

Sugar Loaf Mountain Challenge

Mount Dora—Tavares—Astatula—Ferndale
Montverde —Minneola—Sugar Loaf Mt.
Astatula—Lake Jem—Mount Dora

The Mount Dora Bicycle Festival has invited cyclists to tour the scenic back roads of central Florida for nearly two decades. Organized by the Florida Council of the American Youth Hostels and the Mount Dora Chamber of Commerce, the festival draws more than a thousand cyclists to this charming resort town every October. Blaine Franz, program director for the Florida Council of AYH, is quick to recommend the metric century to Sugar Loaf Mountain as one of the most memorable rides of the weekend.

Thought Florida was flat, did ya? If this is your first tour of central Florida, you may be in for some surprises. Rising to the grand elevation of 310 feet, Sugar Loaf affords a panoramic view of glistening Lake Apopka and various smaller lakes. The entire metric century is a jaunt from one lake to another: Lake Dora, Lake Beauclair, Lake Harris, Little Lake Harris, Grassy Lake, and Lake Jem.

The first leg of the ride departs from Mount Dora with a relaxing sweep alongside Lake Dora. After negotiating through Tavares, the route passes briefly through citrus groves of orange and grapefruit trees where sprawling ranch houses sit in the midst of sand and fruit trees. Marinas and more lakefront homes appear with brief glimpses of Lake Harris. Then, it's on to Astatula and a straight-away on county road 561 for a hookup with the loop around Sugar Loaf Mountain.

From Astatula, the countryside becomes an increasingly rural landscape of pastureland and citrus groves. The atmosphere is one of quiet and solitude, although towns are never far away, and the route crosses major state highways. Unfortunately, the serenity is edged by encroaching urban sprawl. Bold billboards posted by prospective developers sit atop Sugar Loaf and other hilltops in the area. For now the arduous climb to the top of Sugar Loaf Mountain is rewarded by a heady sensation. To gaze far off and downward into a horizon is unusual in Florida. While the abundant beauty of so much water, sunny sky, and lush vegetation easily explains the lure of "the Sunshine State," we fear for the vulnerability of the landscape.

Bicycle tours of the Mount Dora area are best enjoyed in the spring and autumn months. If you do attempt the Sugar Loaf Mountain Challenge in the summer, be sure to carry plenty of water or other fluids. Convenience stores occur with frequency along the route.

Just 25 miles northwest of Orlando, a bicycle tour in the Mount Dora area would be a refreshing way to work out the kinks from a whirlwind tour of Disney World. The Sugar Loaf Mountain Challenge can be spread out over two days with an overnight stay at the Lake Minneola Inn in downtown Minneola. If you haven't time for the metric century, try the shorter, more direct route to Sugar Loaf Mountain. Both rides culminate with the singular view from atop Sugar Loaf Mountain.

The Basics

Start: The ride begins at Donnelly Park on Baker St. in downtown Mount Dora. There are several municipal parking lots along Baker St.
Length: 39.7 or 63.2 miles.
Terrain: Flat to rolling hills.
Food: Convenience stores and restaurants are located in all the

towns and cities along the route. At mile 36, Minneola makes a nice break point.

For more information: Florida Council of the American Youth Hostels, Inc., P.O. Box 533097, Orlando, FL 32853-3097; (407) 649-8761. Mount Dora Chamber of Commerce, Old Seaboard Coastline Dépot, 341 N. Alexander St., P.O. Box 196, Mount Dora, FL 32757; (904) 383–2165.

Miles & Directions

For the 39.7-mile option—

- 0.0 Donnelly Park on Baker St. Proceed north on Baker St.
- 0.1 Left onto Third Ave.
- 0.2 Right onto Tremain St.
- 0.5 Left onto Liberty Ave.
- 0.7 Right onto Grandview St.
- 0.9 Left onto Johns Ave.
- 1.1 Right onto Clayton St.
- 1.9 Right onto Beauclair Rd.
- 2.2 Left onto Dora Dr.
- 4.5 Right onto Sadler Rd. (CR-448 west).
- 6.0 Left onto CR-448A. Use caution at intersection.
- 7.3 Right onto CR-48 west to Astatula.
- 11.8 Left onto CR-561 south. CR-561 is two-laned and has some industrial traffic.
- 14.9 Go straight on CR-455.
- 16.5 Left onto Sugarloaf Mountain Rd.
- 19.9 Left onto CR-561A east.
- 20.6 Left onto CR-455 north.
- 25.2 Right onto CR-561 north.
- 28.3 Right onto CR-48 east (Astatula).
- 32.6 Left onto CR-448A north.
- 34.1 Right onto CR-448 east (Sadler Rd.).
- 35.3 Left onto Dora Dr.
- 37.6 Right onto Beauclair Rd.

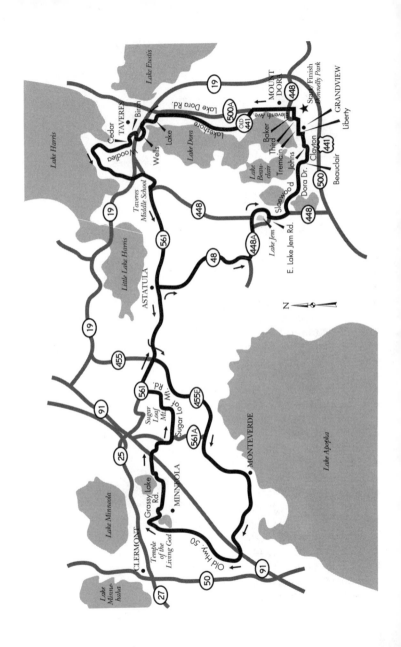

- 37.9 Left onto Clayton St.
- 38.7 Left onto Johns Ave.
- 38.9 Left onto Grandview St.
- 39.1 Left onto Liberty Ave.
- 39.2 Right onto Tremain St.
- 39.5 Left onto Third Ave.
- 39.6 Right onto Baker St.
- 39.7 Donnelly Park.

For the 63.2-mile option—

- 0.0 Donnelly Park on Baker St.
- 0.3 Left onto Eleventh Ave.
- 1.1 Bear left at Y intersection.
- 1.2 Go straight on Old US-441. Old 441 becomes Lakeshore Dr., which later becomes Lake Dora Dr.
- 5.9 Oblique railroad tracks. Use caution. Keep going straight through downtown Tavares.
- 6.7 Left onto Lake Ave.
- 6.9 Right onto Wells Ave.
- 7.1 Left onto Mansfield St., which becomes County Rd. through mobile home park.
- 7.9 Right onto SR-19, going north; stay right but prepare for a quick left turn.
- 8.0 Left onto Birch Blvd.
- 8.1 Left onto Cedar Ave.
- 8.8 Right onto Woodlea Rd., which becomes Lane Park Rd.
- 12.4 Cross CR-19 at Lane Park Rd. Caution: busy intersection.
- 13.1 Right onto CR-561, going south. Tavares Middle School is just before your turn.
- 17.5 Pass the Astatula Community Bldg.
- 19.8 Left onto CR-455, going east.
- 31.8 Right onto CR-455.
- 31.9 Right onto Old Hwy. 50. SR-91 is visible to your right.
- 36.0 Temple of the Living God to your left. (Old Hwy. 50 becomes Washington St. If you continue straight, you will go through Minneola.)

- 36.3 At the Y intersection take a sharp right onto Grassy Lake Rd. (also Rockwell). It will seem as if you are turning back in the direction you came.
- 38.3 Left onto Grassy Lake Rd.
- 39.0 Right onto Grassy Lake Rd.
- 40.1 Right onto CR-561A.
- 41.3 Left onto Sugarloaf Mountain Rd.
- 45.4 Right onto CR-561.
- 47.0 Go straight, crossing CR-455.
- 50.1 Right onto CR-48 east.
- 54.6 Left onto CR-448A.
- 55.4 Right onto E. Lake Jem Rd.
- 55.6 Left onto CR-448.
- 58.3 Left onto Sloewood Dr.
- 59.0 Right onto Dora Dr.
- 61.9 Left onto Johns Ave.
- 62.0 Right onto Grandview Ave.
- 62.3 Left onto Sixth St.
- 63.2 Left onto Baker St. You're back at Donnelly Park.

8

Ocala Horse Country Classic

Silver Springs—Citra—Island Grove—Cross Creek
Micanopy—Flemington—Anthony—Silver Springs

Possum Trot Ranch . . . Dalmur Arabians . . . Sunrise Thorough-breds . . . Dally-Ho Farms . . . Haras Santo Maria de Araras. . . . You're cresting hill after gentle hill. Verdant pastures undulate into the horizon. An Arabian stallion tosses his mane to your right while sleek black quarter horses graze to your left. This can't be Florida, it looks like Kentucky.

The Ocala Horse Country Classic is a near-century ramble past the elegant estates and horse farms surrounding Ocala. A thoroughly scenic route, on very low traffic roads, makes this one of the most relaxing long rides in the book. These roads are so ideal for cycling that they have been incorporated into several popular Florida cycling events: the Horsy Hundred, the MS-150, and the week-long Florida Classical Safari. While the terrain is decidedly rolling, slight grades allow most riders to crest hills without downshifting.

The Ocala Horse Country Classic rewards on other levels as well. Around mile 30 the route stumbles upon Cross Creek and the home of writer Marjorie Kinnan Rawlings. Even if you have not read her Pulitzer prize–winning novel, *The Yearling,* you most likely have seen the MGM movie. Daily tours of Cross Creek poignantly re-create Rawlings's independent choice to pursue her craft in relative isolation.

Her modest house is surrounded by a small grove of orange

trees; she labored hard to maintain a working farm in the 1930s and 1940s, a time when Florida was profoundly less developed. As Rawlings writes in her autobiography, *Cross Creek,* "At one time or another most of us at the Creek have been suspected of a degree of madness. Madness is only a variety of mental nonconformity and we are all individualists here." There is just enough wildness left in the landscape to sense what life must have been like.

Just 10 miles farther along the route, you'll come upon Micanopy, a historic hamlet with two bed and breakfast inns and no less than ten antique shops. Named for Seminole chief Micanopy, downtown Micanopy is sheltered from the bustle of nearby Highway 441 by the shade of massive live oaks draped with Spanish moss.

Micanopy is ideally located along the route for an overnight stay. Why not divide this tour into two days for an outstanding weekend? While the Shady Oak Bed and Breakfast offers country charm, the Herlong Mansion revels in southern elegance. Each room is named (Amber's Suite, Mae's Room, Pink's Room . . .) and decorated with antiques that lend each room a unique character.

If you prefer sleeping under the stars, Paynes Prairie State Preserve offers camping within a mile of downtown Micanopy. This preserve is a unique biological habitat with "twenty distinct biological communities of wet prairie, marsh pine flatwoods, hammocks, swamps and ponds." Naturalist William Bartram passed through the area in 1774. His writings and drawings make note of wildlife still abundant in the preserve, including sandhill cranes, eagles, hawks, waterfowl, wading birds, alligators, and otters.

Once you've completed the loop, you might devote an afternoon to a tour of Silver Springs, famous for its glass-bottom boat rides. Fourteen springs with names like Blue Grotto, Mammoth Spring, and Florida Snowstorm feed crystal waters at the rate of 800 million gallons a day.

The Basics

Start: Begin in downtown Silver Springs at the intersection of SR-40 and CR-35 (Silver Springs and Wild Waters are located on the southeast corner).

Length: 83.8 miles.
Terrain: Flat to rolling hills.
Food: Plan to stop in Micanopy for lunch. Try the Wild Flowers Cafe at 38 miles on Hwy. 441. There are country stores in Cross Creek (28.3 miles) and Flemington (46.6 miles).
For more information: Paynes Prairie State Preserve, Rte. 2, Box 41, Micanopy, FL 32667; (904) 466–3397.

Miles & Directions

- 0.0 Head north on CR-35/N.E. 55 Ave. (Baseline Rd.).
- 1.8 Cross CR-326.
- 4.9 Left onto N.E. 97 St.
- 7.1 Right onto N.E. 36 Ave. (Note the rooster field on your right.)
- 10.3 Right onto N.E. 130/CR-329.
- 11.3 Left onto N.E. 47 Ave.
- 12.8 Right onto CR-316.
- 14.9 Left onto Pine Church Rd./N.E. 175 St. (Pine United Methodist Church is on the corner.)
- 20.1 Right onto N.E. 189 Ave.
- 20.9 Cross CR-318.
- 21.7 Right onto US-301.
- 23.6 Left onto CR-325 (Island Grove).
- 27.5 Alachua County Park on the left.
- 27.6 Marjorie Kinnan Rawlings home.
- 28.3 Turn right after the bridge. Cross Creek flows between Lake Lochloosa and Orange Lake.
- 31.6 Left onto CR-346.
- 36.7 Right onto US-441 (paved shoulder).
- 37.6 Left onto CR-234 (Cholokka Blvd.) into Micanopy.

From the intersection of US-441 and CR-234, you may continue 1.27 miles on US-441 to Paynes Prairie State Preserve.

- 38.1 Right onto CR-234 leaving Micanopy.
- 39.4 Pass through I–75 interchange.

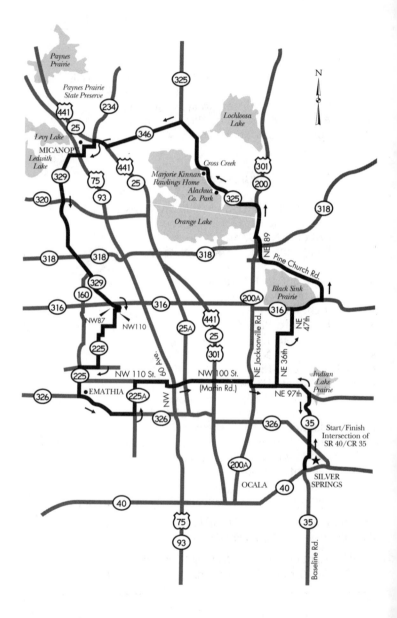

- 41.0 CR-234 becomes CR-329 as you enter Marion County.
- 43.0 Cross CR-320.
- 46.6 Cross CR-318. Town of Flemington.
- 48.9 Cross N.W. 160 St. leading to Le Cheval Farm.
- 50.4 Cross CR-316.
- 51.0 Right onto CR-225.
- 52.9 Left onto N.W. 87 Ave. at Possum Trot Ranch. (Road becomes N.W. 90 Ave.)
- 54.8 Look for camels on your left.
- 55.6 Right onto N.W. 110 St. at T intersection.
- 56.8 Left onto CR-225.
- 58.5 Left onto CR-326, community of Emathia.
- 62.3 Left onto CR-225A. Note the massive sign sporting the logos of horse farms in the area.
- 64.1 Look for llamas on your left.
- 65.8 Right onto N.W. 110 St. at Wooden Horse Stud.
- 67.5 Right onto N.W. 60 Ave.
- 68.4 Left onto N.W. 100 St. (Martin Rd. on map).
- 69.2 Cross I–75 overpass.
- 70.2 Cross CR-25A.
- 72.5 Cross US-301/US-441. (N.W. 100 St. soon becomes N.E. 100 St.).
- 74.9 Right onto N.E. Jacksonville Rd.
- 75.1 Left onto N.E. 97 St. Rd.
- 75.3 Dangerous Y intersection. Bear left across rough railroad tracks.
- 76.6 Pass rooster field on your left.
- 78.9 Right onto CR-35, going south (red-surfaced road).
- 82.0 Cross CR-326 (Oak Rd. on the map).
- 83.8 Back in Silver Springs at the intersection of SR-40 and CR-35 (also known as Silver Springs Blvd. and N.E. 55 Ave.).

9

Tropical Trail Challenge

Titusville—Port St. John—Eau Gallie
Merritt Island—John F. Kennedy Space Center
Merritt Island National Wildlife Refuge—Titusville

The Tropical Trail Challenge is adapted from the Spacecoast Free-wheelers' Intracoastal Waterway Century, which travels alongside the Indian and Banana rivers near Cape Canaveral and Cocoa Beach, Florida. The Spacecoast Freewheelers are best known for their annual Cross Florida Ride, during which cyclists dip their wheels in the Atlantic Ocean; proceed on a one-day, 170-mile exodus across the state; and finally dip their wheels in the Gulf of Mexico. The Tropical Trail Challenge does, in fact, retrace a segment of the Cross Florida route along the Indian River.

The highlight of the Tropical Trail Challenge is the waterfront view available on more than 90 percent of the route. Indian River Drive and the Tropical Trail run right along the river. The Eau Gallie Causeway and the NASA Causeway make wide crossings of the Indian River. The Tropical Trail also runs alongside the salt marshes of the Merritt Island National Wildlife Refuge. Glittering expanses of water beckon for much of the journey.

The Merritt Island National Wildlife Refuge is a birder's paradise. As you pedal west on the NASA Causeway, relishing a stiff tail wind, you might gaze out on wavy cordgrass and black needlerush as a snowy egret takes flight. Birds frequenting the park include ospreys, tricolored herons, gray egrets, blue herons, turkey vultures, and eagles.

Although water presents a vast landscape, this is not a bike ride of wide open spaces. Most of the route travels through residential neighborhoods that occupy nearly every square foot of waterfront. Indian River Drive is a narrow, two-lane road lined with palm trees. The houses along the waterfront are luxurious with their Spanish stucco and Florida pastels. The subtropical landscaping is lush with thick, green lawns and blooming flowers even in winter.

The Tropical Trail Challenge is a special treat from October through March, when most parts of the country are cataloguing shades of brown. Plan a tour of the John F. Kennedy Space Center, then spend an extra day cycling the Tropical Trail Challenge. You'll leave with a charmed view of life in the Sunshine State.

The Basics

Start: Begin at the Port St. John Plaza on US-1 in Port St. John, just south of Titusville.
Length: 76.7 miles.
Terrain: Flat.
Food: There are numerous convenience stores and restaurants along the route.
For more information: Spacecoast Freewheelers, c/o Irvin Hayes, 166-A N. Atlantic Ave., Cocoa Beach, FL 32931.

Miles & Directions

Because of space constraints, many short roads do not appear on the accompanying map. Close attention to the following directions is therefore advisable.

- 0.0 From the Port St. John Plaza parking lot, head south on US-1.
- 1.7 Left onto C-515 (Indian River Dr.).
- 8.8 Go straight on Brevard Ave.
- 9.2 Left onto Oak St. (around the traffic circle).
- 9.4 Right onto Riverside Dr. (Rockledge Dr.).

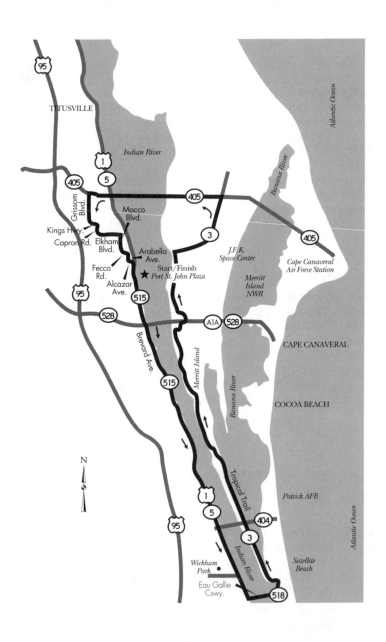

- 15.7 Left onto US-1.
- 23.9 Left onto Pineapple Ave.
- 26.3 Left onto Montreal Ave. (Eau Gallie Causeway) over the Intracoastal Waterway.
- 28.1 Left onto Riverside Dr./South Patrick Dr.
- 29.0 Left onto Banana River Dr.
- 29.5 Right onto South Tropical Trail.
- 39.2 Left onto Crooked Mile Rd. (Be on the lookout for this side street that goes up a hill.)
- 40.4 Left onto South Tropical Trail.
- 46.0 Straight on North Tropical Trail.
- 50.0 Right onto Venetian Way.
- 50.3 Left onto Courtney Parkway.
- 51.0 Left onto Grant Rd.
- 51.3 Right onto North Tropical Trail.
- 56.3 Straight on SR-3 (Courtney Parkway).
- 57.9 Entrance to John F. Kennedy Space Center.
- 61.4 Left onto 405 (the NASA Causeway) at the overpass.
- 70.0 Left onto Grissom Blvd.
- 73.0 Left onto Kings Hwy.
- 74.5 Right onto Capron Rd.
- 75.0 Left onto Elkham Blvd.
- 75.1 Right onto Macco Blvd.
- 75.2 Left onto Fecco Rd.
- 75.6 Straight on Arabella Ave.
- 75.8 Left onto Alcazar Ave.
- 76.1 Left onto Aron Rd.
- 76.6 Right onto West Ave.
- 76.7 Back at the Port St. John Plaza.

Georgia

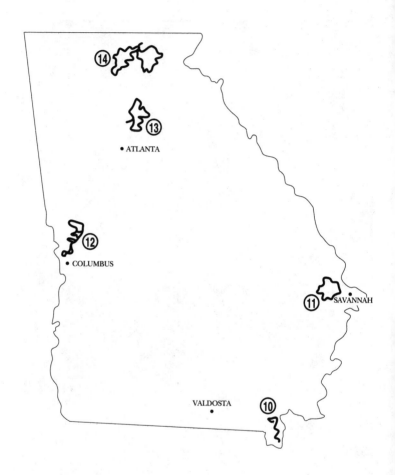

Georgia

10

Okefenokee Swamp Challenge

Bryceville—St. George—Okefenokee National
Wildlife Refuge—St. George—Bryceville

Each spring, members of the North Florida Bicycle Club make a 60-mile migration from Jacksonville, Florida, to the Okefenokee Swamp in southeast Georgia. The Okefenokee National Wildlife Refuge is one of the most exotic natural settings in the Southeast. A habitat for alligator, black bear, bobcat, the bald eagle, the Florida sandhill crane, numerous other waterfowl, mammals, and reptiles, the Okefenokee intrigued visitors well before the European settlers appeared on the scene. "Okefenokee" derives from Indian words meaning "land of the trembling earth."

While the Florida and Georgia back roads approaching the swamp do not tremble, they often shimmer in the heat. The summer months can be relentless with temperatures hovering in the nineties. Spring and fall are the best seasons for cycling to Okefenokee. We've shortened the North Florida Bicycle Club's route a bit, as many area cyclists do, to make a 37.5-mile cruise one way, or a 75-mile challenge round-trip.

Bicycling up to the dark, tea-colored waters of the Okefenokee helps place the vast swamp into perspective with the surrounding area. You cycle along a series of bland country back roads, then—wham! this wild, alligator-infested swamp appears. And we mean infested. The latest official census counted more than 10,000 alligators within the 400,000-acre wildlife refuge.

The route from Bryceville is not without its points of interest. At mile 16 you cross the St. Marys River, the boundary between Florida and Georgia, although this "boundary" is of dubious distinction. Local folk known as "crackers" lend a no-nonsense, free-thinking attitude to the region in both states. The St. Marys is a plaintive, tree-lined river, which slowly carries water from the Okefenokee Swamp to the Atlantic Ocean. This is your first contact with the primeval waters.

Up ahead, the sleepy town of St. George, with its live oak canopies, churches, and small cafés, makes a pleasant stop. Try some catfish at Shirley's Cafe if you're hungry, or sit in the shade with a cool drink. Endless rows of slash and loblolly pines lining the road make the next 15 miles to the swamp desolate and lonely. Boons Creek and Cornhouse Creek cross Highway 301 as they wander toward the Atlantic.

When you reach the east entrance of the Okefenokee National Wildlife Refuge, you'll have just a few more miles of pine barren before the changing landscape begins to reveal itself. Gradually the ground to either side of the road becomes less stable. National Park Service literature describes the swamp as "a vast bog inside a huge, saucer-shaped depression that was once part of the ocean floor." Ancient origins for a landscape with an eerie, prehistoric feel. *Tyrannosaurus* . . . *Brachiosaurus* . . . you can almost see their slow, hulking bodies slogging through the vast expanse of murky water.

Extinct species aside, the Okefenokee Swamp supports a fascinating variety of wildlife. The Florida sandhill crane, the red-cockaded woodpecker, green-winged teal, heron, egret, and ibis all inhabit the refuge. While alligator provide the major excitement, water moccasin, copperhead, and the small, but deadly, coral snake are reptiles found here that make most people squirm. Wildlife displays at the Swamp's Edge Interpretive Center are expert and captivating. The aforementioned snakes and a massive stuffed gator are likely to heighten your senses and put your reflexes on ready alert. It's wise to spend time here before heading out on the nature trails.

The park service has developed Swamp Island Drive, a 4.5-mile, paved nature loop to Chesser Island and the Chesser Island Homestead. The Chesser Island Homestead illustrates the lifestyle of those Georgia crackers we mentioned earlier. A working farm features a house tour and an introduction to turpentine, sugarcane, and ham-curing enterprises. Swamp Island Drive is also the access road to a wooden boardwalk (1.5 miles round-trip) that leads into the swamp where two observation towers enable you to survey the horizon.

This brief loop makes an excellent bike ride if you're content with short distances. There's so much to investigate inside the wildlife refuge that families, or groups, divided between cyclists and noncyclists can find activities appealing to everyone.

There's no point in cycling to the Okefenokee National Wildlife Refuge if you do not plan to devote an hour or two to exploration (and this is a mere glimpse at the park). Ultimately, you must trade bicycles for canoes to travel deep into the swamp. The park has more than 120 miles of canoe and motorboat trails set up for overnight primitive camping.

The Basics

Start: Park at the Bryceville, Florida, post office on Hwy. 301. From I–10 take exit onto Hwy. 301 and go north toward Bryceville. From Folkston, Georgia, follow Hwy. 301 south to Bryceville.

Length: 37.5 or 75 miles. Swamp Island Dr. makes a pleasant 4.5-mile loop within the refuge.

Terrain: Flat to rolling.

Food: The primary restaurants and convenience stores are in St. George around mile 17.5. Try Shirley's Cafe at mile 18. Concession facilities in the park offer juices, soft drinks, and snack food.

Special conditions: The summer climate is extremely humid with temperatures in the nineties. Spring and fall are the best seasons for a tour of the Okefenokee Swamp. Carry a bike lock if you plan to explore the park on foot. You'll need one to secure your bike for the walk to the observation towers along Swamp Island Dr.

For more information: Refuge Manager, U.S. Fish and Wildlife Service, Okefenokee National Wildlife Refuge, Rte. 2, Box 338, Folkston, GA 31537; (912) 496–3331. Park admission fee is $3.00. Visitor hours are 7:00 A.M.–7:30 P.M.

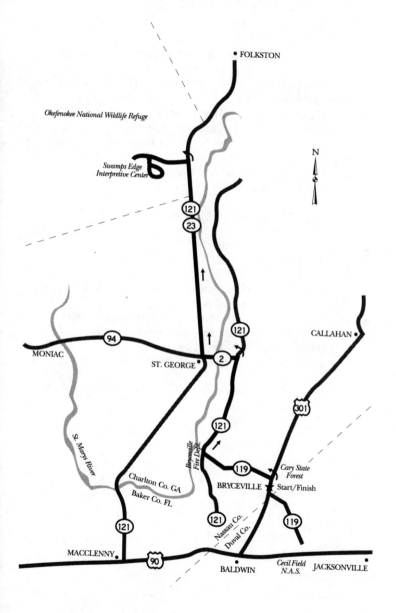

FOLKSTON

Okefenokee National Wildlife Refuge

Swamps Edge
Interpretive Center

N

121
23

94
MONIAC
ST. GEORGE
2
121

CALLAHAN

301

121
Bryceville Fire Dept.

119
BRYCEVILLE

Cary State
Forest
Start/Finish

Charlton Co. GA
Baker Co. FL

St. Marys River

121
MACCLENNY
90

121
Nassau Co.
Duval Co.
119
BALDWIN
Cecil Field
N.A.S.
JACKSONVILLE

Miles & Directions

- 0.0 From the Bryceville Post Office head north on Hwy. 301.
- 0.5 Left onto FL-119.
- 0.8 **Caution: rough railroad tracks.**
- 6.6 Right onto FL-121. Bryceville Fire Department at intersection. FL-121 parallels the St. Marys River, about a mile to the west.
- 14.9 **Caution: more railroad tracks.**
- 15.1 Left onto SR-2 West.
- 15.7 Weigh station.
- 16.7 Cross the St. Marys River and the Georgia–Florida state line.
- 17.4 St. George city limits.
- 17.7 Speed bumps.
- 17.9 Right onto GA-121/23 North.
- 21.2 Cross Boons Creek. You are coming into a few slight hills.
- 32.0 Cross Cornhouse Creek.
- 33.3 Entrance to Okefenokee National Wildlife Refuge; left into the park. The road surface becomes rough pavement.
- 37.1 Speed bumps. Self-serve pay gate.
- 37.5 Swamp's Edge Interpretive Center and parking lot.

For a round-trip excursion simply follow the route back the way you came for a total trip of 75 miles.

11

Sylvania Cruise

Newington—Sylvania
Blue Springs Park—Newington

Bicyclists visiting the historic Savannah riverfront may find themselves wondering where to ride. Mountain bikes prove ideal for the
cobblestone streets outlined in the driving tour of the historic district, but we asked the Coastal Bicycle Touring Club about the *best*
cycling in the area. Ann Glendenning recommended a route forty-
five minutes west of Savannah known as the Transylvania Tour,
and we biked the back roads of Screven County on an overcast December day.

In its path to the Atlantic Ocean, the Savannah River flows in a
southeasterly direction, forming the boundary between Georgia
and South Carolina. The Sylvania Cruise loops through the farmland and pine forests of the coastal plain, stopping midway in Sylvania. Sylvania is located 10 miles from the Savannah River in the
midst of a countryside forested in longleaf, loblolly, and slash pine
dotted with oak and tall magnolia trees in spots.

Rice plantations have predominated in the swamplands along
the Savannah River. Although blackwater swamps edge up to the
road in many spots, we saw no evidence of rice crops. Crops on
land include peanuts and soybean. Hogs, dairy cows, and beef cattle are prominent along the route.

The Sylvania Cruise is a simple, back-roads ride virtually free of
traffic. BRAG, the Bicycle Ride Across Georgia, has passed through
the town of Sylvania many times on the way to Savannah. Sylvania

is typical of friendly small towns all across Georgia that have welcomed BRAG riders for more than a decade.

The winter season does seem to bring out a desolate quality in the landscape. The town of Newington, starting point for the ride, was nearly closed up on the day we passed through. Blue Springs Park is a popular swimming hole in the area, but when we cycled into the park the place was empty.

The seasons most likely change the character of this ride. We passed by deer hunters dressed in camouflage fatigues and bright orange vests. Their three-wheelers roared down dirt roads tracing grids through loblolly pine forest. Camellia bushes provided the only other splash of color with their bright red and pink blossoms.

A gray-colored heron flew abruptly out of the brush as we cycled down Georgia 24 near Crater Lake. Frequent ponds and creeks support geese, ducks, and other waterfowl.

The local chamber of commerce confirms that Blue Springs Park is a hoppin' place in the summer. Just imagine the comfort of that cool spring on a humid summer day. Spring would be ablaze in azaleas and wild dogwood. And fall comes so late to the area that a few oak and maple will still be turning in December.

This 40-mile ride can be cycled as a quick workout or taken at a more leisurely pace. Cruise through Sylvania in search of lunch, then cycle to Blue Springs Park for a swim or a short, quarter-mile walk to the banks of the Savannah River.

The Basics

Start: North of Savannah on I–95, take the exit for GA-21 north. Follow GA-21 north for 35 miles to Newington. The Sylvania Cruise begins at the main intersection in Newington where GA-21 and GA-24 meet.

Length: 40.7 miles.

Terrain: Flat to slightly rolling hills.

Food: Look forward to a break in Sylvania at mile 18, where you will find convenience stores and restaurants. There are very few stores in the surrounding countryside.

For more information: Savannah Area Convention and Visitors Bureau, 222 W. Oglethorpe Ave., Savannah, GA 31499; (912) 944–0456 or (800) 444–2427.

Miles & Directions

- 0.0 Begin in Newington at the intersection of GA-24 and GA-21. Proceed on GA-24 East (Main St.) past the Newington post office.
- 0.3 Bear right on Creek Rd. (CR-250).
- 2.8 Right following pavement on CR-250 (unmarked).
- 3.3 Left at the stop sign on CR-250 (unmarked).
- 4.6 CR-250 bears left (unmarked).
- 5.7 Right at the stop sign on CR-245 (unmarked road).
- 9.1 Ditch Pond Church on left.
- 9.5 Right at four-way stop onto Halcyondale Rd. (CR-245).
- 14.7 Cross Farmdale Rd.
- 16.3 **Caution: railroad tracks at a bad angle.**
- 17.4 Sylvania city limits.
- 17.6 Screven County High School.
- 17.9 Bear left onto S. Main St.
- 18.6 Right onto E. Ogeechee St. (First Union Bank is on the right-hand corner.)
- 20.9 Bear right onto Buck Creek Rd. (CR-238). Note hog farm.
- 25.6 Right onto GA-24 East. (Buck Creek Church is on the left at the intersection.)
- 27.9 Jacksons Creek Church on right.
- 28.5 WASHINGTON SLEPT HERE historical marker on right.
- 35.3 Blue Springs Church on left.

For a side trip to Blue Springs Park, take the road just preceding Blue Springs Church for 1.9 miles. The park may be somewhat unkempt, but a swimming hole fed by Blue Spring is still in use. A short trail will take you to a view of the Savannah River. Picnic tables are available.

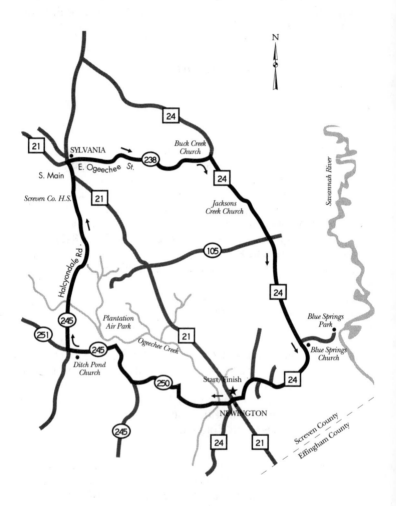

- 39.1 North Newington Baptist Church.
- 40.2 Newington city limits.
- 40.6 **Caution: railroad crossing.**
- 40.7 Back in downtown Newington.

12

Pine Mountain Classic

Columbus—Flat Rock Park—Ellerslie—Waverly Hall
Shiloh—Franklin D. Roosevelt State Park—Durand
Warm Springs—Shiloh—Waverly Hall—Ellerslie
Flat Rock Park—Columbus

The Columbus waterfront sets a slow pace on a Sunday afternoon. The Chatahoochee River ripples quietly past broad, brick warehouses restored from textile mills and a Civil War iron works into office buildings and trade-show exhibit space—a determined effort at preservation for a city a bit off the tourist beat. Why drive to Columbus for the Pine Mountain Classic?

This unassuming pocket of southwest Georgia chronicles a fascinating historic chapter. The Pine Mountain Classic ventures from the northern edge of Columbus into the red clay hills that rise to the north. After skirting railroad tracks for the first 25 miles, the route heads toward Pine Mountain, Warm Springs, and Franklin D. Roosevelt State Park.

Franklin D. Roosevelt's attraction to the natural hot springs in the area is the great curiosity of the ride. While the humble charm throughout the countryside hardly appears spectacular enough to lure a president, a tour through the outdoor treatment pools in the town of Warm Springs illuminates the gravitational force of the artesian hot springs that offered hydrotherapy to polio victims.

President Roosevelt spent considerable time in this area; he visited the springs forty-one times. In 1932 he constructed Little White House outside Warm Springs as a residence for his regular visits. On April 12, 1945, he died in Warm Springs, suffering a massive stroke while his portrait was being painted.

While the Southeast Velo Club bills the Pine Mountain Classic as a one-day tour de force comparable to the Assault on Mt. Mitchell, the Pine Mountain Classic may be more enjoyable as a weekend tour divided by an overnight stay at the Hotel Warm Springs Bed and Breakfast or camping at Franklin D. Roosevelt State Park.

Spending the evening at the Hotel Warm Springs Bed and Breakfast places you in downtown Warms Springs with time to spare for a tour of Little White House and browsing in the numerous gift shops and antique stores. While breakfast at the bed and breakfast promises a rich southern feast of cheese grits, sausage, eggs, biscuits, jams, and gravy, the Victorian Tearoom and the Blue Willow Cafe offer a variety of dining options.

For campers, Franklin D. Roosevelt State Park features plenty of activities perfect for cooling down after an intense morning of cycling. There's lake swimming and hiking along the Pine Mountain Trail. You might set up camp and bicycle into Warm Springs, following the route as it loops around Pine Mountain.

The ride along the ridgeline on GA-190 is the scenic highlight of the route. Views of Pine Mountain Valley and Callaway Gardens make all the climbs worthwhile. The Southeast Velo Club has named the steepest of them "Hyperventilate Hillclimb." It comes at mile 35.1 on the approach to Pine Mountain. The mountain most definitely rises up out of nowhere. Check out the relief map on display at the Information Center in Franklin D. Roosevelt State Park to gain perspective on the area.

The Pine Mountain Classic, held around the third Sunday in April each year, is no Assault on Mt. Mitchell, but it is a rewarding bike ride combining pleasant countryside with challenging terrain and historic points of interest. Spring and fall offer the best climate for cycling in the region.

The Basics

Start: From I–185 take exit 7 north of Columbus. Take the North Bypass (GA-22/80 East). Take exit 6 (Schomberg Rd.). Turn left following signs for Shaw High School. Ride starts from the high school parking lot.

Length: 104.0 miles.

Terrain: Rolling to hilly. The Southeast Velo Club puts it this way: "All hills are less than 1 mile in length. Most are less than 7 percent grade with the exception of one, and it is almost 10 percent."

Food: There are numerous country stores along the route. Look for Oliver's Grocery at 10.2 miles, Verdeman's Grocery at 19.8, Kings Gap Inn at 35.1, and a country store at 65.6. At mile 50, Warm Springs has several restaurants, including the Victorian Tearoom and the Blue Willow Cafe.

For more information: The Southeast Velo Club, 2503 Camille Dr., Columbus, GA 31906; (404) 322–4223.

Miles & Directions

- 0.0 Shaw High School parking lot. Exit left to Schomberg Rd.
- 0.2 Right onto Schomberg Rd.
- 0.3 Left onto East GA-22/80.
- 0.8 Right onto Blackmon Rd.
- 1.4 Left onto Warm Springs Rd.
- 1.8 Flat Rock Park is on the right.
- 5.8 Entering Harris County.
- 8.6 Entering Ellerslie.
- 9.1 Bear left on Warm Springs Rd.
- 10.1 Left onto Harris Rd.
- 14.8 Right onto GA-208 East.
- 17.3 Entering Waverly Hall.
- 18.6 Left onto GA-85 North/GA-208/Alt. US-27. **Caution: busy intersection.**
- 25.7 Bear left onto GA-85 North.
- 26.3 Entering Shiloh.
- 27.7 Downtown Shiloh.
- 28.1 Left onto Kings Gap Rd. **Caution: railroad crossing.**
- 35.1 Kings Gap Inn.

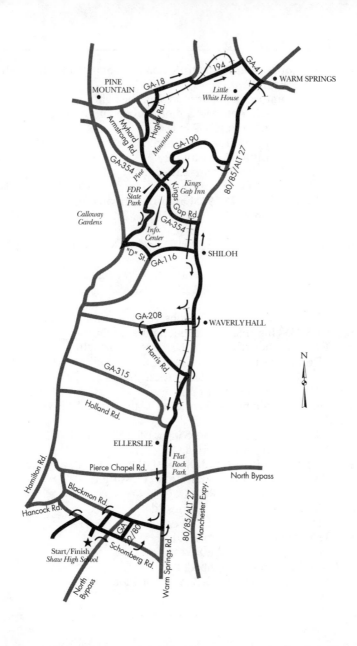

- 35.7 Entrance to Franklin D. Roosevelt State Park. Get ready for a downhill run.
- 36.2 Swimming and picnic area on the right.
- 36.4 Bear right onto Myhard Armstrong Rd.
- 37.0 Right onto Hugley Rd.
- 39.0 **Caution: railroad crossing.**
- 39.2 Right onto GA-18 East.
- 41.7 Cross White Sulphur Creek.
- 43.0 Entering Durand.
- 43.7 Right onto GA-194. **Caution: railroad crossing.**
- 49.1 Right onto GA-41 South/Alt. US-27.
- 49.2 Entering Warm Springs.
- 50.0 Right onto GA-85. Warms Springs shops and restaurants at this intersection.
- 50.5 Little White House entrance on the right.
- 53.7 Right onto GA-190.
- 56.8 Dowdell's Knob.
- 58.5 Entering Franklin D. Roosevelt State Park.
- 62.6 FDR Information Center, nature exhibit.
- 64.3 Overlook of Callaway Gardens on the right.
- 65.6 Sharp left onto D St. Prepare to descend.
- 68.0 Left onto GA-116 East toward Shiloh.
- 76.0 Enter Shiloh.
- 76.3 **Caution: railroad crossing.** Right onto GA-85W/ GA-116.
- 78.0 Go straight onto GA-85/Alt. US-27 South.
- 84.5 Entering Waverly Hall.
- 85.2 Right onto GA-208 West (becomes Alexander Dr. through town). **Caution: railroad crossing.**
- 88.8 Left onto Harris Rd.
- 93.1 Right onto Warm Springs Rd.
- 94.8 Enter Ellerslie.
- 102.3 Right onto Blackmon Rd.
- 103.6 Left onto GA-22/80 West.
- 103.7 Right onto Schomberg Rd.
- 104.0 Enter Shaw High School parking lot.

13

North Georgia Wine Country Challenge

Lawrenceville—Chateau Elan Winery
Chestnut Mountain Winery
Auburn—Dacula—Lawrenceville

With Atlanta sprawling in every direction, the woodsy countryside of Gwinnett County is a refuge for area bicyclists. The Gwinnett Touring Club sponsors the annual Fine Whine Tour, which rambles through the countryside while visiting two of the six wineries in North Georgia: Chateau Elan and Chestnut Mountain. These north Georgia wineries cultivate and harvest vinifera grapes to produce a variety of wines including Chardonnay, Cabernet Sauvignon, Riesling, Chenin Blanc, and Merlot.

The North Georgia Wine Country Challenge adopts 46- and 57-mile routes from several popular club rides through the area. While the wineries add a touch of extravagance with the promise of wine tastings and gourmet lunches, the rolling to hilly terrain, past grassy pastures of horse and cattle ranches, is reason enough to enjoy this ride.

Small subsistence farms manage to retain their charm in spite of the chaos speeding past on nearby I-85. Then again, evidence of a world curiously awry is as close as nearby Braselton—the town acquired recently by the actress Kim Basinger. A chat or two with natives of this area introduces friendly, industrious folk just a bit overwhelmed with the growth of Atlanta. The mixture of natives and suburbanites is evident all along this tour. Families that have farmed large tracts for generations finally sell out, and neat grids of middle-class houses sprout up in their place.

There are several lavish estates along the route. Down Camp Branch Road sprawl modern tributes to southern architectural styles. Chateau Elan Winery is a re-creation of a sixteenth-century French chateau looking grandly incongruous with the surrounding red clay hills. For those with quiet sensibilities, Chestnut Mountain Winery is refreshing in its total lack of pomposity. Its mile-long driveway winds through woods along a hard-packed gravel road where deer and fox forage freely.

The North Georgia Wine Country Challenge is best approached as an all-day tour of the countryside. Allow yourself plenty of time for lunch at Chateau Elan, or pack some crusty French bread and an assortment of cheese for a picnic on the grounds of either winery. You will arrive at the wineries at mile 27 and 29, so be sure not to overdo it. There are several tough hills, and at least 20 miles to go, on the back side of the route.

Visitors to the area have their choice of accommodations in the Atlanta area. If you're here to do Atlanta, by all means stay in the city and drive out for the bike ride. If you would just as well avoid the congestion of Atlanta, seek out the more relaxed atmosphere of Lawrenceville. The flourishing town here since 1821 is doing just fine, thank you, in spite of Atlanta. Try the County Seat Cafe for tasty comfort foods like meatloaf, sweet potato soufflé, and baby-back ribs.

The Basics

Start: The ride begins outside Lawrenceville at Dyer Elementary School. From I–85 take GA-316 past exits for Lawrenceville about 6 miles. Turn left onto Hurricane Shoals Rd. Dyer Elementary will be to the left at this turn.
Length: 46.5 and 57.0 miles.
Terrain: Rolling to hilly.

Food: Numerous country stores line the route. Most notable are Hog Mountain Store at 8.0, Spout Springs Superette at 18.3, Kountry Korner Store at 42.8, and Chip's General Store at 44.6. At 27.5 Chateau Elan offers a gourmet lunch, but be prepared to wait.

For more information: Gwinnett Touring Club, c/o Danny Linton, P.O. Box 597, Grayson, GA 30221; (404) 962–8153.

Miles & Directions

- 0.0 Start at Dyer Elementary School. Proceed left on Hurricane Shoals Rd. (Hurricane Shoals Rd. passes through an industrial park.)
- 3.4 Left onto Old Peachtree Rd.
- 4.9 Right onto Old Fountain Rd. NE.
- 6.4 Left onto SR-324 NE.
- 8.0 Cross SR-124 NE.
- 9.4 Cross I–85.
- 9.5 Right onto Camp Branch Rd. NE.
- 10.7 Right onto Wallace Rd. NE. (Wallace Rd. becomes Ridge Rd.)
- 12.0 Cross Hamilton Mill Rd. NW. Go straight on Ridge Rd.
- 13.0 **Caution: speed bumps.**
- 13.1 Cross Thompson Mill Rd. NE.
- 14.8 Cross Friendship Rd. (Ridge Rd. becomes Hog Mountain Rd.)
- 18.3 Right onto Spout Springs Rd.
- 21.1 Left onto Union Circle.
- 22.4 Right onto Union Church Rd.
- 25.0 Right onto Old Winder Hwy.
- 27.5 Entrance to Chateau Elan Winery on the right.
- 28.2 Cross I–85.
- 28.5 Right onto SR-124.
- 29.0 Entrance to Chestnut Mountain Winery on the right. Proceed 0.75 miles down a hard-packed gravel road.
- 32.2 Left onto Dee Kennedy Rd. NE.

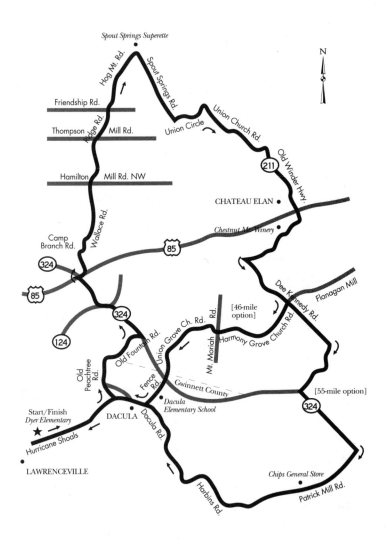

Spout Springs Superette

Hog Mt. Rd.

Spout Springs Rd.

Union Church Rd.

Friendship Rd.

Ridge Rd.

Thompson   Mill Rd.

Union Circle

Old Winder Hwy.

Hamilton   Mill Rd. NW

211

CHATEAU ELAN

Wallace Rd.

Chestnut Mt. Winery

Camp Branch Rd.

85

324

85

Dee Kennedy Rd.

Flanagan Mill

324

[46-mile option]

124

Old Fountain Rd.

Union Grove Ch. Rd.

Mt. Moriah Rd.

Harmony Grove Church Rd.

Old Peachtree Rd.

Fence Rd.

Gwinnett County

Dacula Elementary School

[55-mile option]

324

Start/Finish
Dyer Elementary

★

DACULA

Dacula Rd.

Hurricane Shoals

LAWRENCEVILLE

Chips General Store

Harbins Rd.

Patrick Mill Rd.

N

For the 46.5-mile option:

- 34.4 Right onto Harmony Grove Church Rd.
- 35.8 Auburn city limits.
- 36.3 Cross Mt. Moriah Rd. (Harmony Grove Church Rd. becomes Union Grove Church Rd.)
- 37.4 Union Grove Church Rd. becomes Fence Rd. when you enter Gwinnett County.
- 39.2 Cross SR-324 NE.
- 41.8 Dacula Elementary School on the left.
- 42.0 Right onto Dacula Rd.
- 42.4 Left onto Old Peachtree Rd.
- 43.0 Left onto Hurricane Shoals Rd.
- 46.5 Back at Dyer Elementary School.
- 36.2 Cross the county line/Auburn Rd.
- 36.7 Right onto Bee Maxey Rd.
- 37.5 Right onto Carl-Cedar Hill.
- 38.8 Carl city limits.
- 39.0 **Caution: railroad tracks.**
- 39.1 Left onto SR-324/GA-8.
- 41.4 Right onto Patrick Mill Rd.
- 43.8 Cross SR-316.
- 45.0 Cross into Gwinnett County. Patrick Mill Rd. becomes Harbins Rd. SE.
- 50.5 Cross SR-316.
- 50.8 Dacula city limits.
- 51.5 Cross US-29. (Harbins Rd. becomes Dacula Rd.)
- 52.5 Cross Fence Rd.
- 52.9 Left onto Old Peachtree Rd.
- 53.6 Left onto Hurricane Shoals Rd.
- 57.0 Back at Dyer Elementary School.

14

Dahlonega
"Six Gap" Classic

Dahlonega—Neels Gap—Jacks Gap—Unicoi Gap
Helen—Hogpen Gap—Vogel State Park
Wolfpen Gap—Woody Gap—Dahlonega

The Bicycle Association of North Georgia has engineered a rugged roller coaster ride through the foothills of the Blue Ridge Mountains that's sure to challenge the best you've got to offer. The red clay hills surrounding Dahlonega and Helen are full of legend and history. If you have a colorful imagination, you might roll out of downtown Dahlonega to the echoing riffs of "Dueling Banjos"—the lively banjo melodies picking up speed and intensity as you go. James Dickey's back-woods characters, made famous by the movie *Deliverance,* were inspired nearby along the Chattooga River.

In 1828 Dahlonega became the capital of the first major gold rush in the United States. The name "dahlonega" is derived from the Cherokee word meaning "yellow metal." Before or after the ride, be sure to spend some time in the Dahlonega Courthouse Gold Museum to learn about the gold rush and view coins minted in Dahlonega and gold nuggets mined from the area.

From Dahlonega, at 1,450 feet, the century route heads out to conquer six mountain gaps ranging in elevation from Hogpen Gap at 3,490 feet to Unicoi Gap at 2,949 feet. The route crosses the Appalachian Trail at Brasstown Bald, Hogpen Gap, and Woody Gap. By the time you've finished, you will have climbed and descended more than 10,300 feet each way. There's as much down as up, with plenty of thrilling descents in store. Sharp, hairpin turns on narrow, mountain roads require caution and confident bike-handling skills. In its history the Six Gap has been marred by one serious bike accident caused by brake failure on a descent.

While this classic presents the greatest challenge as a single-day event, several highlights along the route make it well suited for an overnight tour. Helen, Georgia, is a touristy town with shops and a Bavarian village that would provide amusements for an overnight stay.

Vogel State Park off GA-180 makes an outstanding base camp for the ride. With the route mapped out as a figure eight, Vogel State Park sits near the midway point and makes an ideal starting point. You could explore each half of the figure-eight at your leisure beginning from the park. This approach is made even more appealing since Dahlonega falls midway on one loop and Helen sits midway on the other.

The Basics

Start: Park in the commuter parking lot of North Georgia College along S. Church St.
Length: 99.2 miles.
Terrain: Hilly to mountainous. You will climb more than 10,300 feet and descend the same distance. Some of the descents are hairy. Please use extreme caution.
Food: Although this is a long ride, the facilities are well spaced along the route. The first major eating establishment is Turner's Corner Restaurant at 14.8 miles. In the next segment of the ride there are country stores at 22.1, 27.3, 30.3 and 49.8 miles. The city of Helen is up ahead at 51.4. There are a wide variety of restaurants here including several serving German food. There are additional stores at 69.4, 78.8, 82.7, 83.2 and 91.7 miles.
For more information: Bicycle Association of North Georgia, c/o Peech Keller, 18025 Union Hill Rd., Alpharetta, GA 30201; (404) 751–1061.

Miles & Directions

- 0.0 From the commuter parking lot of North Georgia College, turn right onto S. Church St.
- 0.2 Right onto W. Main St. Bear right around the courthouse following GA-52 East.
- 1.0 Left following GA-52 East.
- 1.2 Bear right following GA-52 East.
- 2.3 Left onto Rockhouse Rd. (unmarked road). Miss Scarlet's Revenge Antiques is on the corner. Use caution.
- 4.5 Left onto Porter Springs Rd. (unmarked).
- 4.6 Cross Cavender Creek Rd. Continue on Porter Springs Rd. Cavender's Creek Baptist Church on right.
- 10.7 Right onto US-19 North.
- 14.8 Left onto US-19 North/US-129 North.
- 16.7 Entering Chattahoochee National Forest.
- 18.9 De Soto Fall Recreation Area.
- 19.6 Roadside park on left.
- 22.5 Neels Gap.
- 25.6 Go straight, crossing GA-180 East.
- 27.9 Right onto GA-180 East.
- 35.1 Entrance to Brasstown Bald. Cross Appalachian Trail.
- 40.3 GA-17/GA-75 South. Signs to Unicoi State Park.
- 42.9 Unicoi Gap. Prepare to descend.
- 51.4 Helen city limits.
- 51.6 Right onto Hamby St.
- 51.7 Right onto Escowee Dr./Ridge Rd.
- 51.9 Bear left, following Ridge Rd. uphill.
- 53.1 Left onto GA-75 Alt.
- 54.5 Right onto GA-348 (Richard Russell Scenic Highway).
- 60.6 Overlook to Raven Cliffs Wilderness Area.
- 61.6 Hogpen Gap. Cross Appalachian Trail.
- 68.5 Left onto GA-180.
- 69.4 Left onto US-19/US-129/GA-180.
- 71.7 Right onto GA-180 West (Wolfpen Gap Rd.).
- 77.8 Bear right on GA-180 West.
- 81.9 Enter Suches.

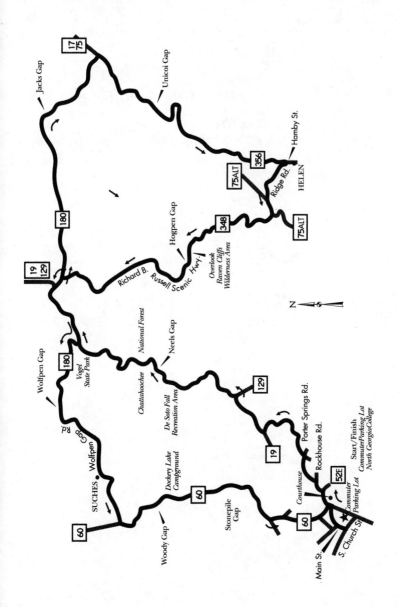

- **82.7** Left onto GA-60 South.
- **84.7** Woody Gap. Cross the Appalachian Trail.
- **94.6** Right onto GA-19/GA-69 South.
- **98.8** Right following GA-19/GA-60 South. Follow the circle around the courthouse.
- **99.1** Right onto Church St.
- **99.2** You're back at the North Georgia College parking lot.

Mississippi

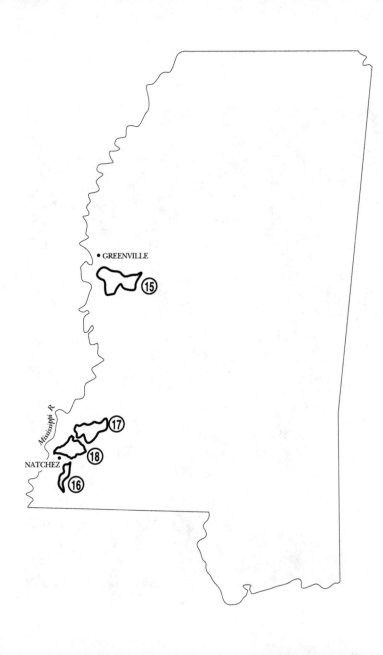

Mississippi

15

Mississippi Delta Cruise

Leroy Percy State Park—Mount Holly Plantation
Yazoo National Wildlife Refuge—Hollandale
Leroy Percy State Park

The Mississippi Delta Cruise should be cycled while humming a classic blues tune like Robert Johnson's "Hellhound on My Trail." This is, after all, the landscape immortalized by William Faulkner in the novels *As I Lay Dying* and *Go Down Moses*. Hard labor in oppressive heat and humidity spawned a special brand of music, the "Delta Blues." As you cycle through the Mississippi Delta, the more fanciful clichés and southern notions you've been entertaining will trickle away like slow-sliding beads of sweat. If you find yourself out on Highway 1 on a sweltering July day, well, that's all the better. Generations of farmers have toiled under the very same conditions. It's a quality of heat that never changes—thick, sticky, strength-sapping heat.

The landscape is dominated by a handful of agricultural enterprises. The principal crop has been, and still is, cotton—"King Cotton," as it's called. The newer, booming industry is catfish. Ponds, methodically laid out in hues of unnatural greens, breed thousands of catfish, which, fried or blackened, are a Mississippi treat.

Throughout this ride you know and sense the presence of the mighty Mississippi, although you never quite see the river. You can spot the tree line that hugs the riverbed and disappears into the horizon, but the only way to see the river from the loop is to detour in the direction of the fishing villages scattered along Highway 1.

The ride originates in Leroy Percy State Park, Mississippi's oldest state park. There you'll find swimming and gator-watching, two activities that go naturally with the heat. If you require more refined accommodations, the Mount Holly Plantation is more than happy to offer refuge from the heat. With their lavish bed and breakfast accommodations, you can enjoy the privileges so few in the area had one hundred years ago.

Surrounded by all the cotton and catfish, Yazoo National Wildlife Refuge offers sanctuary to birds, deer, and other native wildlife.

The Basics

Start: Park at the visitor center inside Leroy Percy State Park.
Length: 38.6 miles.
Terrain: Flat.
Special conditions: Bring your insect repellent and *plenty* of water—remember, the humidity can be very oppressive.
Food: Stores are not well spaced along the route. You should be able to get a drink at Mount Holly Plantation, around 13.8 miles. The only other stores are located near the end of the route in Hollandale, at 32.6.
For more information: Leroy Percy State Park, P.O. Box 176, Hollandale, MS 38748; (601) 827–5436.

Miles & Directions

- ■ 0.0 Leroy Percy State Park.
- ■ 0.3 Right onto MS-12 West.
- ■ 7.8 Left onto MS-1 South.
- ■ 13.8 Mount Holly Plantation and Bed and Breakfast.
- ■ 18.6 Left onto MS-436 East.

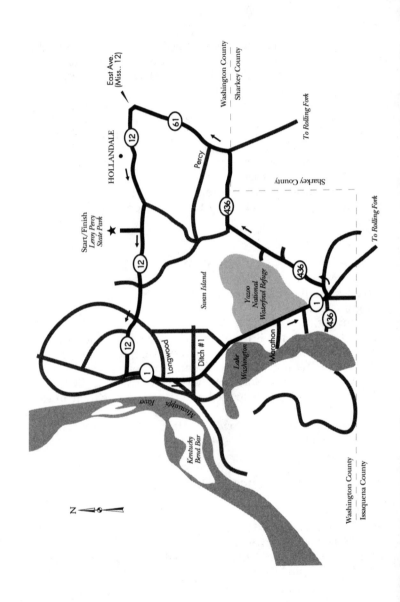

- 22.6 Yazoo National Wildlife Refuge.
- 28.0 Left onto MS-61 North toward Hollandale.
- 32.6 Entering Hollandale, Miss. Left onto East Ave. (MS-12).
- 33.4 Left onto MS-12 West.
- 38.6 Right at the sign for Leroy Percy State Park.

16

Church Hill Cruise

Coles Creek Picnic Area—Mount Locust
Emerald Mound—Church Hill
Springfield Plantation—Coles Creek Picnic Area

The Church Hill Cruise pleasantly eases you back into history. From the Natchez Trace Parkway to the plantation row of Mississippi Highway 553, you simply roll along hoping to absorb huge chunks of the Old South, life-styles that live on in the past tense of lore and legend.

The artifacts are very real and tangible. Your first stop is Mount Locust, an inn or stand, restored by the National Park Service, that offered refuge to travelers along the Old Trace. Mount Locust grew from a basic cabin in the 1700s to a seven-room house as the Ferguson family prospered into the 1800s. The massive oak, poplar, and hickory trees that shade the vast grounds surrounding the inn are a refuge now, and surely were then, from the oppressive summer heat. Rest rooms and water are also available here.

From Mount Locust you head south on the parkway to Loess Bluff. From this overlook, windblown topsoil from the Ice Age is formed into a high bluff. This ancient soil is found in deposits all along the Mississippi River in sections 3 to 30 miles wide.

From the Ice Age, cruise a few more miles and shift your thinking to the prehistory of A.D. 1300. Emerald Mound is a dramatic man-made structure covering nearly eight acres. Even if your imagination is dulled by the heat, you're likely to conjure up images of sacred Indian ceremonies as you stand atop this site. Gatherings at this mound predate the named tribes of the area: the Choctaw, Chickasaws, and Natchez.

From Emerald Mound, Mississippi Highway 553 rolls its way into the 1800s of the antebellum South. As you pedal along, you will catch glimpses of six plantation houses: The Cedars, Lagonia, Oak Grove, Richland, Springfield Plantation, and Woodland. The Cedars, Lagonia, and Springfield Plantation are open to the public. If you have time, tour at least one of the plantations to experience the segment of history that typifies the Old South for so many.

In the center of all this history, you will encounter the town of Church Hill, aptly named for Christ Church, which sits atop the hill. Built in the 1790s, Christ Church is the oldest Episcopal church in the state. Grave sites of parishioners from the 1800s and 1900s surround the church, pressing in from all sides. Across the road, Wagner's Store is still in operation. If you're friendly, and you hang out for a while, you can hear about the state of the cotton crop and the butter beans and tomatoes. You'll hear stories about hunting quail, wild turkey, and white-tailed deer.

Church Hill Cruise is more about history than bicycling, but what better vehicle for time travel?

The Basics

Start: Park at Coles Creek Picnic Area, milepost 17.5 on the Natchez Trace Parkway. Water and rest rooms are available here. From Natchez, Mississippi, take US-61 to the southern terminus of the Natchez Trace Parkway.
Length: 23.2 miles.
Terrain: Flat to rolling hills.
Food: Country stores across from Emerald Mound at 8.0 miles, Wagner's Store in Church Hill at 13.8, and Brown's Grocery on MS-553 at 14.7.
For more information: Natchez Bicycling Center, 344 Main St., Natchez, MS 39120; (601) 446–7794.

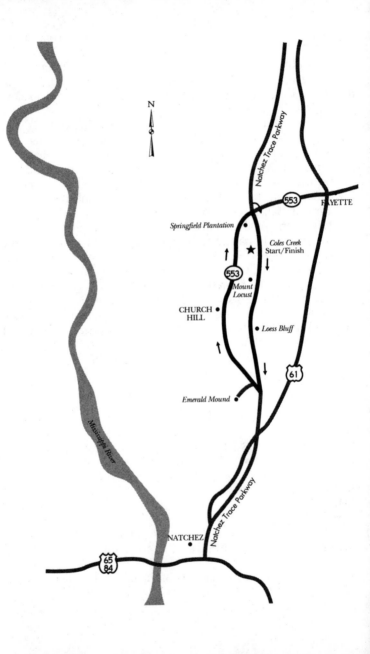

Miles & Directions

- **0.0** Coles Creek Picnic Area at milepost 17.5 on the Natchez Trace Parkway. Head south on Natchez Trace Parkway.
- **1.9** Mount Locust.
- **5.1** Loess Bluff Overlook.
- **7.1** Turn right onto MS-553 following signs for Emerald Mound.
- **7.2** Road forks. Emerald Mound is 0.8 mile to the left. The loop bears right on MS-553.
- **13.8** Entering Church Hill.
- **18.5** Springfield Plantation (open for tours).
- **20.2** Left onto ramp to Natchez Trace Parkway.
- **20.4** Left onto Trace heading south.
- **23.2** Back at Coles Creek.

17

Windsor Ruins Cruise

Port Gibson—Windsor Ruins
Natchez Trace Parkway—Port Gibson

The Corinthian columns of Windsor Ruins may represent the atmosphere of the Old South better than a tour of the antique-filled antebellum homes of Natchez. Remnants of a fire in the 1860s, the columns are all that's left of a once grand mansion. With kudzu threatening to overtake the scene, the columns are a reminder of how colorful, yet temporal, this chapter of American history is.

Dale Hart, leader of Classic Bicycle Tours, makes a point to lead his tours off the Natchez Trace Parkway on a detour exploring the historic sites of Port Gibson and Windsor Ruins. In 1863 Gen. Ulysses S. Grant called Port Gibson "the town too beautiful to burn." Happily for those of us anxious to pedal past its historic churches and homes, the town was made a Union headquarters in the Civil War and was spared from damage.

This pleasant, 30-mile loop begins in downtown Port Gibson, following the "Windsor-Battlefield Tour" route, which quickly becomes canopied by oaks and Spanish moss. The winding, hilly course provides just enough challenge to stimulate your appetite for a picnic lunch in the shade of oaks and hickories surrounding Windsor Ruins. There are no facilities for miles, so plan to pack a snack or two.

After a break at the ruins, the route meanders through kudzu jungle to the Natchez Trace Parkway. You'll enjoy a 7-mile stretch along this straightaway before exiting back toward Port Gibson.

The Windsor Ruins Cruise is perfect for those enjoying an overnight stay in Port Gibson. The elegant Oak Square Plantation and Bed and Breakfast on Church Street would make the perfect refuge for a leisurely weekend. An evening spent sleeping in canopied beds, then a southern breakfast served amid antiques from the eighteenth and nineteenth centuries, and finally an exploration of the countryside by bicycle—all would truly immerse you in an Old South experience.

The Basics

Start: Park at the Port Gibson Visitors Center on Hwy. 61 in downtown Port Gibson.
Length: 30.5 miles.
Terrain: Flat to rolling.
Food: There are almost no stores along the route. We suggest packing snacks for a picnic at Windsor Ruins. At 29.2 miles you'll find a Shell station and store.
For more information: Port Gibson-Claiborne County Chamber of Commerce, P.O. Box 491, Port Gibson, MS 39150; (601) 437–4351.

Miles & Directions

- 0.0 From Port Gibson Visitors Center turn right onto Hwy. 61 North (Church St.).
- 1.4 Left onto Carroll St.
- 1.7 Left onto Rodney Rd.; follow signs toward Windsor Ruins.
- 5.7 Point Lookout.
- 11.6 Windsor Ruins. Follow a short gravel driveway to the foot of the ruins.
- 13.3 Keep straight, do not bear right. This road becomes MS-552 East.
- 14.3 Bethel Church, circa 1826.
- 15.2 Claremont Plantation.

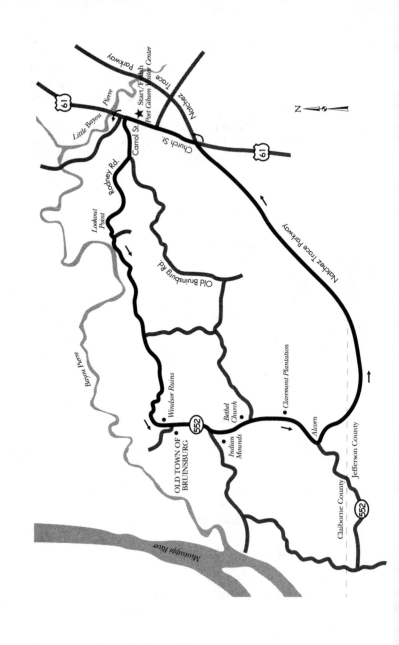

- 21.5 Left onto entrance ramp for the Natchez Trace Parkway.
- 21.7 Left onto Natchez Trace Parkway heading north.
- 28.6 Right onto exit ramp for Hwy. 61.
- 28.8 Left toward Port Gibson on Hwy. 61 North.
- 30.5 End at Port Gibson Visitors Center.

18

Rosswood Plantation Cruise

Natchez Trace Parkway—Fayette—Redlick
Lorman—Natchez Trace Parkway

Daniel Murphy, of the Natchez Bicycling Center along Main Street in downtown Natchez, Mississippi, recommends the Rosswood Plantation Cruise and the Church Hill Cruise as among the best rides in the area. In fact, as a native of the state, Daniel feels the Natchez area offers some of the best cycling in all of Mississippi. We would have to agree.

While the Church Hill Cruise condenses Old South history, from Indian to antebellum in 20 miles, the Rosswood Plantation Cruise takes you a little bit farther off the beaten path. The route passes through a working rural landscape that actually comes closer to the realities of life in the contemporary South.

You'll begin on the Natchez Trace Parkway but quickly head off on rolling back roads toward Fayette, Mississippi. Fields of soybean, corn, cotton, and winter wheat extend for miles, while modest houses dot the roadside. Many of the simple, clapboard houses appear to be in decline. Abandoned cars and rusted farm equipment keep company with wildflowers and brambles. You pass businesses like DJ's Chicken House and J. W. Costley General Merchandise. If "Deep South" has a landscape, this may be it. The humidity is thick, and a myriad of insects drone on and on.

The sprawling Rosswood Plantation strikes a stark contrast to the modest homes of the area. Built in 1857, the elegant, classic revival home has been restored to its original splendor. The plantation is open as a bed and breakfast and welcomes bicyclists. Dale Hart, director of Classical Bicycle Tours, treats his touring groups to a luxurious evening here.

From Rosswood Plantation the route heads toward Lorman and the Old Lorman Country Store and Museum. Built in 1890, the Lorman Country Store is a novelty and a curiosity, with "edge-grain long-leaf pine floorings." At some point the practice of displaying business cards got out of hand, and you can roam the nooks and crannies of the store reading more than thirty thousand business cards of visitors from around the world. For bicyclists, the country store offers a wide variety of snack foods as well as a respite from the heat.

The final leg of your journey winds down along the Natchez Trace Parkway. Be sure to watch for white-tailed deer and wild turkey. The latter may well squawk and fly into the brush upon your arrival.

Daniel calls the Rosswood Plantation route "a true flashback from one hundred years ago." We wonder—is it a flashback, or has time stood still in rural Mississippi?

The Basics

Start: Park at the Coles Creek picnic area on the Natchez Trace Parkway, located between the 17- and 18-mile markers.
Length: 41.5 miles.
Terrain: Flat to rolling.
Food: You'll find country stores in Fayette at 10.5 miles and Lorman at 26.4.
For more information: Natchez Bicycling Center, 344 Main St., Natchez, MS 39120; (601) 446–7794.

Miles & Directions

- 0.0 Head right from Coles Creek picnic area on the Natchez Trace Parkway.

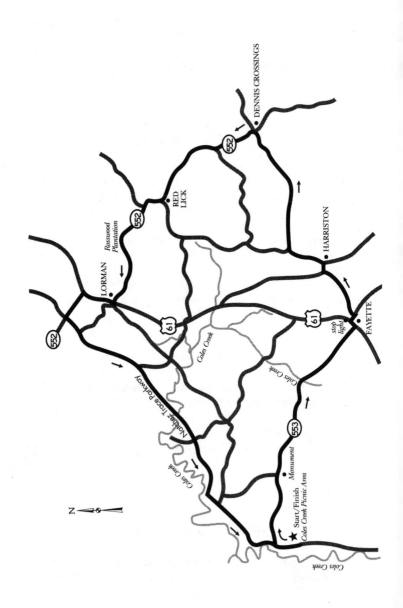

- 2.7 Turn right off the Natchez Trace Parkway onto a cloverleaf that leads you to Hwy. 553.
- 2.8 Turn left onto Hwy. 553 going toward Fayette.
- 5.8 Bridge over South Fork of Coles Creek.
- 10.0 Stop sign at junction of Hwy. 61. Go straight on Hwy. 553 into town of Fayette.
- 10.5 Stop light; turn left.
- 10.9 Turn right and cross over bridge.
- 13.0 Stop sign; turn left. This stretch of road is a little bumpy and has a couple of hills. Just take it easy, because it gets better real soon.
- 14.2 Continue on the same road. Do not take the left fork in the road.
- 18.4 Stop sign (Dennis Crossings). Turn left onto Hwy. West 552.
- 21.0 Entering community of Red Lick. Continue along Hwy. 552.
- 23.9 Rosswood Plantation and Christmas tree farm. Open for bed and breakfast.
- 26.4 Stop sign in Lorman. Proceed left (north) on Hwy. 61. Stay single file, and ride to the right of the roadway.
- 27.6 Turn left onto Hwy. West 552 toward Alcorn State University.
- 28.4 Turn left onto ramp leading to the Natchez Trace Parkway.
- 28.6 Stop sign. Turn left onto Natchez Trace Parkway.
- 33.3 Pass over the North Fork of Coles Creek.
- 38.8 Continue straight on the Natchez Trace past Hwy. 553.
- 41.5 Coles Creek Picnic area and the end of the ride.

North Carolina

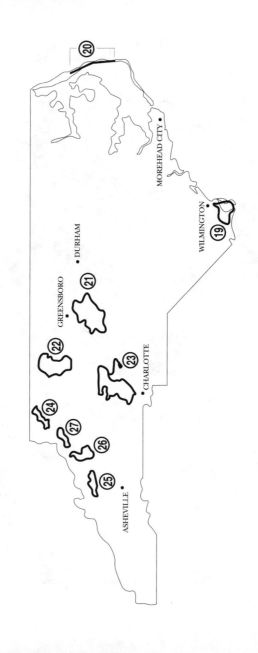

North Carolina

19

Cape Fear Challenge

Wilmington—Carolina Beach—Kure Beach
Southport—Orton—Pinelevel—Clarendon
Belville—Wilmington

In the 1960s movie thriller *Cape Fear,* Robert Mitchum stalks Polly Bergen and Gregory Peck through bald cypress knobs and marsh grass to terrorize them aboard a houseboat on the Cape Fear River. Maybe you saw the 1991 remake where Robert DeNiro stalks Jessica Lange and Nick Nolte through bald cypress knobs and marsh grass. . . . Charged by the suspense of the big screen, you may want to discover the Cape Fear Coast for yourselves.

This ride acquaints you with nearly every aspect of the Cape Fear area. It progresses from city to riverbank to beachfront. And as if a thirty-minute ferry ride were not diversion enough, there are five distinctive points of interest along the way: Fort Fisher and the North Carolina Aquarium in the first half of the loop; Southport, Brunswick Town State Historic Site, and the Orton Plantation Gardens in the second half. You could easily spend hours at each of these places. For a full-fledged weekend getaway, you might consider making this ride a two-day tour with an overnight stay at one of the bed and breakfast inns in Southport.

This loop begins at Chandler's Wharf in the historic district of downtown Wilmington. Heading out of Wilmington, past blocks of restored houses dating back to the early 1800s, the route quickly leaves downtown to meander parallel to the river. In the first 4 miles, the route travels through the thick of the industrial waterfront past massive tank farms and busy loading docks. Once beyond this congestion, River Road is framed by cattails and marsh grass, which lead to the river.

From River Road you climb a bridge over the Atlantic Intracoastal Waterway into Carolina Beach. In Carolina Beach and Kure Beach, the road passes every variety of beach dwelling. Tiny, pastel cottages, smiling with secrets from an endless procession of summer guests, sit next to modern, gray-stained condominiums that sprawl along the oceanfront. The natural beauty of the windswept trees at Fort Fisher rivals that of the most ambitious beach houses.

The ferry ride to Southport, besides offering a welcome break from cycling, provides a nice contrast. Leaving land, the ferry affords a glimpse into the coastal life-style foreign to many landlocked cyclists. Ferries run every fifty minutes, and the crossing takes approximately thirty minutes. The fee for one bicycle and rider is $1.00. Just in case you're planning on coming back the way you came, keep in mind that the last ferry of the day leaves Southport at 6:00 P.M.

Happily, this tour places you in Southport just in time for lunch. There are several cafés and restaurants specializing in seafood. A cruise down Main Street is like pedaling into a Norman Rockwell painting. For a split-second there, you've never heard of index shifters, and instead of reaching for brake levers, you're telling your feet to back pedal into coaster breaks. You'll want to linger here and explore the side streets lined with white clapboard houses shaded by expansive live oak trees.

From Southport you are jolted forward and backward in a time warp. First you fast forward past the Carolina Power and Light Nuclear Power Plant. From there it's 10 miles to Brunswick Town and the Orton Plantation Gardens.

It would be unfortunate to miss the Brunswick Town State Historic Site. First established in 1726, the town boasts a history that spans from colonial times to the Civil War. A walking tour leads from the brick foundation of St. Philips Church along Second Street past the stone and brick foundations of numerous houses. Front Street moves alongside the river to the massive, earthen walls of Fort Anderson. Fort Anderson was built by the Confederacy to protect the Cape Fear River leading to Wilmington.

Adjacent to Brunswick Town, the Orton Plantation Gardens display the extravagant beauty of a southern plantation complete with azaleas, camellias, rhododendron, magnolia, and exotic ornamentals. In the midst of such delicate beauty, you may even spot something dangerous and untamed—like a scaly gator sunning himself near the Chinese bridge.

The final miles can get very steamy in the summer months. We cycled this loop on a Fourth of July weekend when temperatures exceeded 95 degrees. Fortunately, there are two country stores strategically located on the way back to Wilmington.

The final challenge of this tour is negotiating the bridge over the Cape Fear River just before exiting into downtown Wilmington. With a metal grating, and considerable traffic, it demands your best cycling skills. If you can manage a glimpse to your left as you cross the bridge, an excellent view of the Wilmington waterfront and the battleship USS *North Carolina* will bring your impressions full circle.

The Basics

Start: The entrance to Chandler's Wharf on N. Front St. in downtown Wilmington. You'll find parallel parking all along Front St.

Length: 55.8 miles.

Terrain: Flat with possible head winds. Slight climbs over two bridges.

Food: There are plenty of stores and eating places in Carolina Beach, Kure Beach, and Southport. You might look forward to a snow cone at 24.3 miles while waiting to board the ferry. Try a gourmet lunch at the Turtle Cafe at 26.7 miles in downtown Southport. There are two country stores along Hwy. 133.

Special conditions: If you plan to spend time off the bike sightseeing, bring your insect repellent. The mosquitoes are unrelenting at Fort Fisher, the Brunswick Town State Historic Site, and the Orton Plantation Gardens.

For more information: Cape Fear Coast Convention and Visitors Bureau, 24 N. Third St., Wilmington, NC 28401; (800) 222–4757.

Miles & Directions

- 0.0 From Chandler's Wharf entrance on N. Front St. head south away from downtown Wilmington.
- 1.4 Bear right onto Burnett Rd. **Caution: In the next 1.5 miles you will cross three severe sets of railroad tracks. Proceed with extreme caution.**
- 3.0 Turn right onto Shipyard Blvd.
- 3.1 Make an immediate left onto River Rd. **Caution: There are five more bad railroad tracks ahead.**
- 15.3 Turn right onto Hwy. 421 South. This is a four-lane highway with considerable traffic. There is a brief climb over the bridge across the Atlantic Intracoastal Waterway (there is no shoulder).
- 16.4 Bear right off the bridge. Turn right at the sign for Carolina Beach State Park; this is Dow Rd. (1573). Follow Dow Rd. all the way to Kure Beach. (Dow Rd. becomes K Ave. when it bears left just before the sign announcing Kure Beach.)
- 20.5 Turn right onto Hwy. 421 South. This portion of Hwy. 421 is two-laned and congested with beach traffic. Be aware of cars parked parallel to the highway.
- 22.5 Fort Fisher is on your right.
- 22.8 The North Carolina Aquarium at Fort Fisher is off to your left.
- 24.3 Entrance to the Southport/Fort Fisher Ferry.
- 24.3 Proceed off the ferry onto the exit road leading to Hwy. 211.
- 25.3 Turn left onto the junction to Hwy. 211 (1528) toward Southport.
- 26.7 Downtown Southport. The route travels through the center of town.
- 28.1 Turn right onto Hwy. 87.
- 31.4 Go straight on Hwy. 133 North; Hwy. 87 turns left.
- 38.9 Turn right at the entrance to Orton Plantation Gardens. If you visit the gardens, you may have to dismount your bike and walk; the road inside the grounds is made of loose dirt.
- 39.7 The road rejoins Hwy. 133.

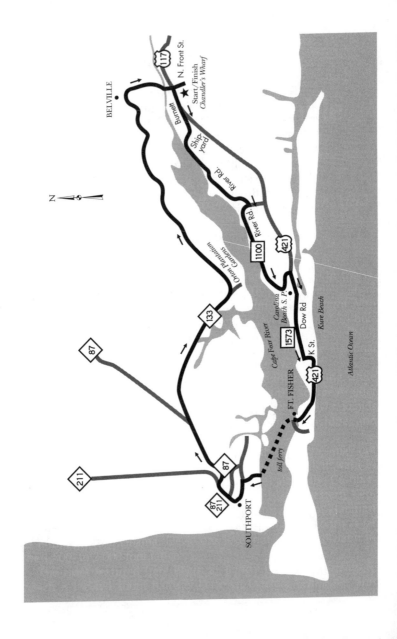

- 52.3 Approaching the town of Belville, look for signs to Hwy. 17 North. Proceed with great care—this is the most heavily traveled road on the route. It has a decent shoulder, but beware of semi-truck traffic. Hwy. 17 crosses the Cape Fear River before you exit into downtown Wilmington. **Use caution when crossing the metal grating in the center of the bridge.** (You could walk your bike across the bridge. There's a narrow shoulder.)
- 55.0 Take the first exit off the bridge, labeled "State Ports Exit."
- 55.2 Turn left onto N. Front St.
- 55.8 Back into historic downtown Wilmington, you have come full circle to Chandler's Wharf.

20

Outer Banks Cruise

Ocracoke—Hatteras—Frisco—Buxton
Frisco—Hatteras—Ocracoke

Landlubbers need not apply. You must roll your bicycle off mother earth, across a steel ramp, and onto one of three ferries to undertake the Outer Banks Cruise. Your ride begins on Ocracoke Island, the southernmost island of the Cape Hatteras National Seashore. In the course of the ride, you hop a ferry to Hatteras Island and make a turnaround at Cape Hatteras Lighthouse.

The Cape Hatteras museum makes a great destination with its portrayal of the U.S. Life-Saving Service at the turn of the century. The lifesaving attempts to rescue crews from shipwrecks are incredible. An explanation of the various fishing methods and native wildlife allow for a greater appreciation of life in the area.

Part of the barrier islands that make up the Outer Banks off the coast of North Carolina, Cape Hatteras National Seashore oversees a land mass in a state of flux. The islands were created by the drag and pull of the Atlantic Ocean, and their shape continues to change. Each island has its own historic lighthouse: Ocracoke Lighthouse, Cape Hatteras Lighthouse, and Bodie Island Lighthouse—all in danger of being reclaimed by the sea.

Cycling in the Outer Banks is all sand and surf. As you cycle down Hwy. 12 (the only highway traversing the Outer Banks), sand dunes and sea oats rise on the Atlantic side. Low brush and twisted cedar trees inhabit the roadside bordering Pamlico Sound. While the ocean is not visible at every moment, its force and rhythmic power is ever present. You cycle along on these narrow, windswept, salt-stung islands unable to dismiss the low roar of Neptune.

Ocracoke Island and Bodie Island are the most pleasant for cycling—much of Hatteras Island is congested and overdeveloped. The best cycling is on Ocracoke, where a fishing-village atmosphere still prevails.

Ocracoke Island has a history of isolation. Traces of Elizabethan speech have been documented in lifelong residents. Animals have their curiosities, too. On the northern end of Ocracoke, be sure to visit the Ocracoke Pony Pasture along Highway 12. The ponies are descendants of the Spanish mustang. Their exact origin on the island is subject to debate, but they once roamed wild and numbered nearly a thousand.

This ride ventures from Ocracoke Island to adjacent Hatteras Island for a trip to the famous Cape Hatteras Lighthouse. From the lighthouse, it's back the way you came; there is no true loop ride. You could meander through the village streets if you like exploring. It would be difficult to lose your way.

National Park Service Ranger Warren Wrenn cautions about traffic on holiday weekends, throughout the summer, and especially on Sunday afternoons, advising bicyclists to avoid travel on Highway 12 during these times. Spring and fall are the best periods for a cycling trip of the Outer Banks. If you can plan a trip exclusively during weekdays in the off-season, touring the entire length of Cape Hatteras National Seashore and on to historic Kitty Hawk would be an outstanding bicycle tour.

While touring bikes are fine, mountain bikes may be the bike of choice at the seashore. There are countless trails off Hwy. 12 marked OTR (or "off-road trails"). While these are intended for four-wheel drive, they make great mountain bike trails. These trails meander out into the dunes and salt marshes for miles. Maps are available from the park service.

The Outer Banks Cruise is broken up by a forty-minute ferry ride aboard one of four Hatteras ferries: the *Kinnakeet*, the *Albemarle*, the *Conrad Wirth*, or the *Frisco*, which run every thirty minutes (every fifteen in the summer months). Relax and flirt with the sea gulls and terns. And when you gaze out at the surf fishermen dotting the coastline, remember, bicycling is just one of many ways to experience the Outer Banks.

The Basics

Start: Ocracoke Village is at the southern tip of Ocracoke Island. You could drive south on Hwy. 12, but it's more fun to take the two-and-a-half-hour ride on the Swan Quarter Ferry. Bring a picnic and a deck of cards or a good book. The Swan Quarter Ferry runs twice a day, departing at 9:30 A.M. and 4:00 P.M.; reservations are essential, as they also are for camping on Ocracoke Island. Parking is available in the village.

Length: 27.8 to Cape Hatteras Lighthouse; 55.6 out and back.

Terrain: Flat with prevailing winds blowing northeast. **Beware of occasional sand blown onto the road.**

Food: There are numerous cafés and restaurants in each of the four towns you pass through: Ocracoke at 0.0 miles, Hatteras at 14.7, Frisco at 19.1, and Buxton at 24.7. Make sure your water bottles are full when you leave Ocracoke. The northern half of Ocracoke Island is all wildlife. You might pack juice or fruit for the ferry ride to Hatteras Island.

For more information: Cape Hatteras National Seashore, Route 1, Box 675, Manteo, NC 27954.

Miles & Directions

- 0.0 Roll your bike off the Swan Quarter Ferry and you're in Ocracoke Village. Proceed north on Hwy. 12 (it's two-laned with no shoulder).
- 0.5 A sign marks a quarter-mile side trip to Ocracoke Lighthouse.
- 4.3 Entrance to Ocracoke Campground.
- 8.4 The Ocracoke Pony Pasture is to your left.
- 14.7 Entrance to the Ocracoke-Hatteras Ferry. (A schedule is posted; no fee.)

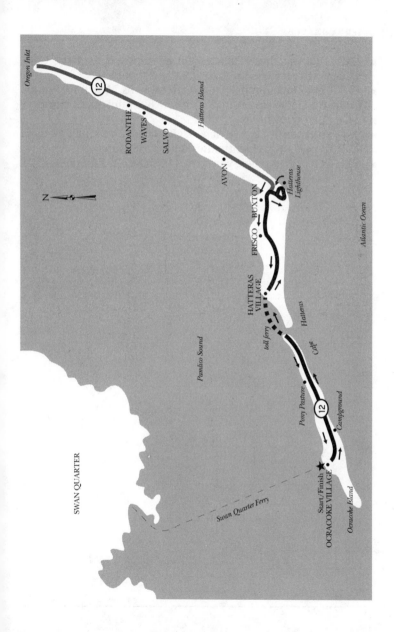

- 14.7 That was short. Hatteras Village is just off the ferry. Continue north on Hwy. 12 (there is a slight shoulder).
- 19.1 Frisco town limits; the shoulder widens. Watch for bumps in the shoulder—unfortunately they're like mini–speed bumps.
- 24.7 Buxton town limits.
- 26.8 Entrance to Cape Hatteras Lighthouse and campground.
- 27.8 Cape Hatteras Lighthouse. Retrace the route.
- 55.6 You're back where you started in Ocracoke Village.

21

Hagan-Stone Cruise

Hagan-Stone Park—Climax—Julian—Whitsett
Gibsonville—McLeansville—Hagan-Stone Park

The North Carolina Piedmont spans 125 miles between the coast and the mountains. The rolling farmland of this area produces soybean, corn, hay, all manner of produce, and North Carolina's most famous crop: tobacco. Just at the frenzied peak of the growing season, when the air above the asphalt shimmers with heat, three-hundred-plus riders brave Dog Daze, an annual bicycling event sponsored by the Triad Wheelers Bicycle Club.

Dog Daze routes follow the back roads of Guilford and Alamance counties. The Hagan-Stone Cruise explores the 50-mile route through Whitsett and Gibsonville, quiet towns that have sprung up around textile mills. Both towns manage to retain an Americana atmosphere although the urban sprawl of Greensboro and Burlington is fast approaching.

From Hagan-Stone Park the route travels to the crossroads of Climax (named for its location on high ground) and Julian. Here the Piedmont Spur of the North Carolina bicycle route system parallels Dog Daze along Hwy. 62. The green-and-white bicycle signs numbered "2" designate this route. Developed by the state bicycling program, these routes create a network of recommended bicycling roads throughout the state (see "State Bicylcing Maps" in the Appendix for information).

From Julian the route continues along NC-62 to Whitsett, Gibsonville, and McLeansville. From town to town the countryside is occupied by dairy farms, Christmas tree farms, greenhouses, and pastureland. An occasional tobacco barn sits dilapidated, its wooden structure and rusted tin roof sagging inward upon itself. Here and there churches and cemeteries capture the imagination with their Civil War dead amid slender, forgotten tombstones weathered to the point of anonymity. Low's Lutheran Church, Freidens Lutheran Church, and Peace Lutheran Church all trace their roots back to the 1700s.

Back roads like these showcase the changes of each season. A crisp, fall day, surrounded by a bright, Carolina-blue sky, would make an outstanding weekend ride. You could set up base camp at Hagan-Stone Park and spend a full day wandering the countryside. Make Gibsonville your lunch destination, with a detour off the route to the shops along Main Street.

Spring is an equally appealing season with daffodils, tulips, and wildflowers in bloom at the many farms and houses along the way. If you find yourself eager to experience the route as the Triad Wheelers intended with Dog Daze, try the Hagan-Stone Cruise in July or August with the cicadas and crickets droning at their feverish pitch.

The Hagan-Stone Cruise is perfect for anyone who enjoys touring the countryside in simple appreciation of the land: There is no famous landmark or natural phenomenon—just pleasant, rolling countryside. Bike the Hagan-Stone Cruise to enjoy the unfolding of your favorite season.

The Basics

Start: Hagan-Stone Park. Follow the signs for the park on US-421 South. US-421 South diverges off of I–40 at the eastern end of Greensboro.
Length: 50.0 miles.
Terrain: Rolling hills.
Food: Country stores and/or restaurants are available in Climax at 3.8 miles, Julian at 6.7, Whitsett at 21.6, Gibsonville at 23.9, and McLeansville at 33.0.

Miles & Directions

- 0.0 Exit Hagan-Stone Park, right onto Hagan-Stone Park Rd.
- 0.6 Left onto NC-22.
- 3.5 Left onto NC-62 North. At this turn you merge with the Piedmont Spur of the N.C. bicycle route. Note the bicycle signs.
- 3.8 Entering Climax, N.C.
- 5.9 Cross US-421.
- 6.7 Entering the town of Julian. Right following NC-62.
- 7.0 Left following NC-62 North.
- 13.1 Cross Alamance Church Rd. The bike route turns right toward Chapel Hill.
- 15.0 Left onto NC-61 North toward Gibsonville.
- 15.2 Low's Lutheran Church (established in 1771) on the left.
- 16.8 Shillelagh Golf Club on the right.
- 21.2 Cross I–40. **Caution: watch for truck traffic.**
- 21.4 Truck stop on right.
- 21.6 Entering Whitsett.
- 22.3 Cross NC-70.
- 23.1 Right following NC-61 North.
- 23.9 Entering Gibsonville.
- 24.8 Right following NC-61 North.
- 24.9 Left following NC-61 North.
- 26.8 Freidens Cemetery (dating from 1745) on the right.
- 26.9 Left onto Freidens Church Rd. Freidens Lutheran Church is on the right.
- 33.0 Entering McLeansville.
- 33.1 Left onto McLeansville Rd.
- 35.1 Cross NC-70; road becomes Mt. Hope Church Rd.
- 35.3 Right onto Clapp Farms Rd.
- 37.3 Right onto McConnell Rd.
- 38.0 Left onto Youngs Mill Rd.
- 40.8 Right onto Mill Point Rd.
- 41.5 Left onto Presbyterian Rd. (bear left at Y). **Caution: dangerous intersection.**
- 41.9 Left onto Alamance Church Rd.

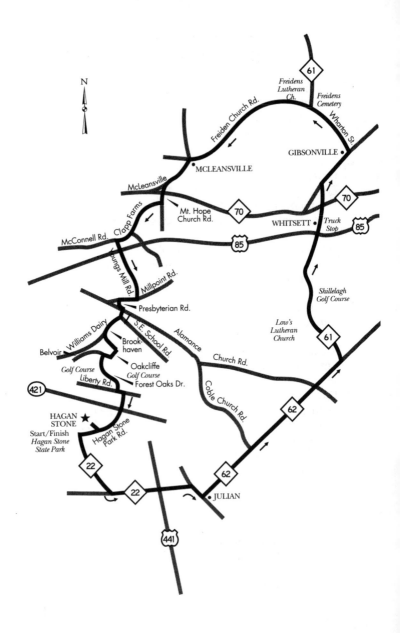

- 42.0 Right onto Southeast School Rd.
- 42.1 Right onto Williams Dairy Rd.
- 43.3 Left onto Brookhaven Dr.
- 44.8 Right onto Oakcliffe Rd.
- 45.5 Right onto Belvoir.
- 45.7 Left onto Forest Oaks Dr. (golf course to left).
- 47.2 Left onto Liberty Rd., then right onto Hagan-Stone Park Rd.
- 47.6 Cross US-421.
- 50.0 Hagan-Stone Park entrance to right.

22

Hanging Rock Challenge

Rural Hall—Germanton—Germanton Winery
Danbury—Hanging Rock State Park
Poplar Springs—Rural Hall

Hanging Rock State Park is the major destination for several popular Winston-Salem bicycling events. The Double Hump Century, pioneered by Ken Putnam of Ken's Bicycle Shop, tackles the two major summits of the area: Hanging Rock and Pilot Mountain. Members of Piedmont Flyers bicycle club make yearly excursions to Hanging Rock State Park.

Hanging Rock is a jagged peak prominent in a range of mountains called the Sauratowns. The Sauratown Mountains stand nearby but apart from the Blue Ridge Mountains, and for that reason they have been called "the mountains away from the mountains." Indeed, the bike ride to the top of the state park features outstanding views of the Blue Ridge Mountains to the west.

The Hanging Rock Challenge features a 37.5-mile loop around Hanging Rock beginning in Rural Hall, a community just north of Winston-Salem. The route passes by rolling, Piedmont farmland planted primarily in corn and tobacco. This ride could be dubbed the "Tobacco Barn Ramble." Every hillside seems to feature a rusty barn at some level of decline. Some barns shelter firewood stacked floor to roof, others are stuffed with hay. Tobacco-curing barns sit stout and square protecting massive, golden brown leaves.

Ty Witt, of Peloton Bicycles, grins menacingly as he reminisces about riding strategy approaching the city of Danbury. First-timers get charged with the rolling descent on Highway 8 from Germanton to Danbury. From a long straightaway it's a fast pack that's confident and surprised by the wall that rises up just before the Danbury city limits.

Established in 1849, Danbury dubs itself "the gateway to the mountains." It's a seemingly remote gateway along the Dan River. If you've chosen a leisurely pace, dismount and peek in a few shop windows. Danbury is the county seat of Stokes County. You'll pass the public library and the county jail just up the road.

The land becomes less developed as you near the six thousand acres protected by Hanging Rock State Park. The road up into the park makes for a very steep climb. While standing on your pedals, you can distract yourself by studying the wildflowers, blueberries, rhododendron, and mountain laurel that grow along the mountainside. Hanging Rock State Park features camping, lake swimming, and hiking along a trail system that passes by several creeks and waterfalls. Rock climbing is also a popular activity in the park.

The 2-mile ascent into the park is optional for this tour. A concession stand operates in the summer from Memorial Day through Labor Day. From the entrance to the park, the route heads west and south back to Rural Hall. Look forward to an overall descent back to your starting point.

Unfortunately, Germanton Winery and Vineyards appears early at mile 4 in the ride. You might save your visit for the end of the tour. Do stop in for a wine tasting and tour of the art gallery, featuring North Carolina artists.

While the Hanging Rock Challenge makes a rigorous day trip, if you're eager to devote a weekend to the area's natural riches, you'll find ample camping and lodging options. The state park allows camping year-round. The newly opened Singletree Inn offers camping as well as bed and breakfast accommodations just 2 miles from the park. You might try beginning this loop from Hanging Rock with Rural Hall and the Germanton Winery as your midway destination. Whichever you choose, Hanging Rock and the Sauratown Mountains will reward with natural beauty and challenging terrain.

The Basics

Start: From US-52, take the Rural Hall exit following NC-66 North 4 miles to downtown Rural Hall. Parking is available along the downtown thoroughfare.

Length: 37.5 miles.

Terrain: Rolling hills to mountainous.

Food: Country stores are well spaced along the routes. Try Manuel's Restaurant at 16.7 miles or lunch at the Singletree Inn around mile 23.5. There are several country stores on the back side of the loop: John Brown's Country Store at 29.1, Hill's Grocery at 29.4, and Tucker's Superette at 32.2. Don't forget to stop for a wine tasting at Germanton Winery at mile 4.0.

Miles & Directions

- 0.0 From downtown Rural Hall head left on NC-65 (Rural Hall–Germanton Rd.).
- 1.1 **Caution: rough railroad tracks.**
- 3.6 Follow NC-8 North through Germanton.
- 4.0 Germanton Winery and Vineyards on the left.
- 4.2 **Caution: rough railroad tracks.**
- 4.5 Left onto NC-8 North.
- 4.6 **Caution: rough railroad tracks.**
- 9.6 Excellent views of the Sauratown Mountain ridge line to the left.
- 11.3 NC-8 North bears right.
- 14.1 Left onto NC-8 North/NC-89 West. Follow signs to Hanging Rock State Park and Danbury.
- 17.3 Entering Danbury. It's uphill through town.
- 19.2 Left onto Hanging Rock Park Rd.
- 20.3 Hanging Rock looms ahead.
- 20.7 Right onto Moores Springs Rd. The entrance to Hanging Rock State Park is just ahead (it's a 2-mile climb to the top of the park). Note the N.C. Bicycling Highway signs.
- 22.5 The entrance to Singletree Inn is to the right. (Follow signs

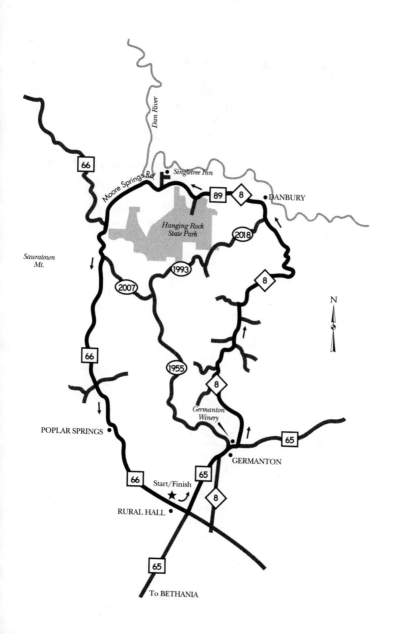

1 mile to the inn. There's a half-mile portion on steep, gravel road.)
- 22.9 Left onto NC-66 South. This intersection is not marked. (Note the N.C. bike route turns right.)
- 27.1 Bear right on NC-66 South.
- 29.7 Pilot Mountain is visible to the right.
- 34.1 Poplar Springs.
- 36.2 Left following NC-66 South. **Caution: busy intersection.**
- 37.0 Entering Rural Hall.
- 37.5 Downtown Rural Hall.

23

Lake Norman Challenge

Denver—Catawba—Lake Norman—Denver

Smack dab in the middle of summer, several hundred North Carolinians converge upon the sleepy mill town of Denver for the best picnic ride of the year, the Lake Norman Excursion. It's the brain child of Dwight Callaway and the Lake Norman Bicycle Touring Club. The organizers must surely have been under the influence of the sixties hit song "Hot Fun in the Summertime."

This ride would be enjoyable all year-round. The back roads of Catawba and Iredell counties are as charming as their names: Grassy Creek Road, Black Snake Road, Joe Johnson Road, Sherrills Ford Road, Monbo, Molly's Backbone, and Buffalo Shoals Road. The route passes by cornfields, tobacco farms, cow pastures, and their proud homesteads, all welcoming with their fresh paint, sunny perennials, grapevine wreaths, and other country accents. One thing's for sure, Molly must have had quite a backbone to inspire the curvature of her road.

If you like rolling hills, this ride's for you. And just to keep us all honest, we'd better add that there are a few steep hills. Dwight Callaway knows the value of this training ground. He placed thirty-ninth in the Paris-Brest-Paris in 1987, going on to compete in the Race Across America in 1988. Knowing the drive required to undertake ultramarathon events, it's refreshing to get to know this down-to-earth cyclist. "The Lake Norman Excursion is just one big picnic," Dwight says, and he's not fibbing. Cantaloupe, oranges, watermelon, a picnic lunch at the end, and friendly North Carolina cyclists make for a day filled with camaraderie.

The Lake Norman Excursion (here renamed the Lake Norman Challenge) is designed for riders of all abilities. It has two options: 43 and 61 miles. A 40-mile option, not covered here, hooks up with the 61-mile option to make a complete century. With so many options, this ride adapts to your energy and ambition.

The Basics

Start: Callaway's Mobile Homes in downtown Denver on Hwy. 16.
Length: 43.0 or 61.0 miles.
Terrain: Rolling hills with a few short, steep climbs.
Food: You'll find stores in Denver at 0.0 miles, Catawba at 21.4, and Skippers Marina at 36.3.
For more information: Lake Norman Bicycle Touring Club, Rte. 2, Box 711, Denver, NC 28037; (704) 483–3940.

Miles & Directions

- 0.0 Leave Denver on Hwy. 16 North.
- 1.8 Right onto Grassy Creek Rd. (1372).
- 3.9 Right onto Hwy. 150.
- 4.2 Left onto Mt. Pleasant Rd. (1849).
- 5.2 Left onto Lineberger Rd. (1851).
- 7.0 Right onto Mt. Beulah Rd. (1846).
- 7.3 Left onto Little Mt. Rd. (1815).
- 9.3 Right onto Joe Johnson Rd. (1817).
- 13.7 Left onto Sherrills Ford Rd. (1848).
- 16.9 Right onto Murry Mill Rd. (1003).
- 19.0 Right onto Hwy. 10.
- 21.4 Downtown Catawba; continue straight ahead.
- 22.2 Left onto Hudson Chapel Rd. (1004).
- 26.6 At Bill's Marina the routes diverge.

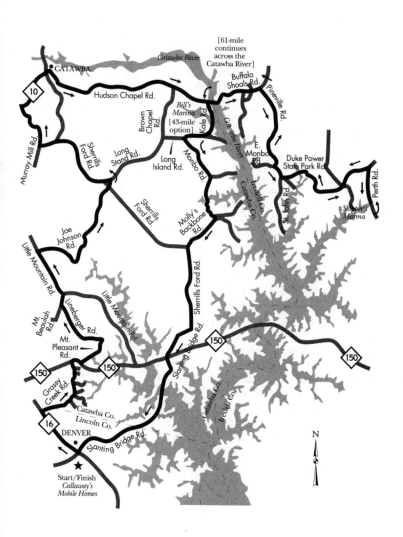

[61-mile
continues
across the
Catawba River]

Catawba River

CATAWBA

10

Hudson Chapel Rd.

Murray Mill Rd.

Brown Chapel Rd.

Buffalo Shoals Rd.

Pineville Rd.

Bill's Marina [43-mile option]

Kale Rd.

Catawba River

E. Monbo Rd.

Duke Power State Park Rd.

Sherrills Ford Rd.

Long Stand Rd.

Long Island Rd.

Monbo Rd.

St. John Rd.

Perth Rd.

Sherrills Ford Rd.

Iredell Co.
Catawba Co.

Sloopers Marina

Joe Johnson Rd.

Molly's Backbone Rd.

Little Mountain Rd.

Little Mountain Rd.

Sherrills Ford Rd.

Mt. Beaulah Rd.

Lineberger Rd.

150

Mt. Pleasant Rd.

150

Slanting Bridge Rd.

150

150

Grassy Creek Rd.

Catawba Co.
Lincoln Co.

Catawba Co.
Iredell Co.

16

DENVER

Slanting Bridge Rd.

★ Start/Finish
Callaway's
Mobile Homes

N

For the 43-mile option—

- 26.6 Right onto Kale Rd. (1832).
- 27.8 Right onto Long Island Rd. (1833).
- 28.7 Left onto Monbo Rd. (1885).
- 30.0 Right onto Molly's Backbone Rd. (1835).
- 32.7 Left onto Sherrills Ford Rd. (1848).
- 36.3 Right onto Slanting Bridge Rd. (1844).
- 42.6 Back in downtown Denver for the finish.

For the 61-mile option—

- 26.6 Cross Lake Norman continuing on Hudson Chapel Rd. which becomes Buffalo Shoals Rd. (1004).
- 28.3 Right onto Pineville Rd. (1332).
- 30.7 Right onto E. Monbo Rd. (1328).
- 30.9 Left onto St. John Rd. (1402).
- 32.5 Left onto Duke Power State Park Rd., past the state park.
- 35.2 Right onto Perth Rd. (1303).
- 36.3 Skippers Marina. Turn around here, and continue back in the direction you came.
- 37.4 Left onto State Park Rd. (1321).
- 41.0 Right onto St. John Rd. (1402).
- 41.6 Right onto E. Monbo Rd. (1328).
- 41.8 Left onto Pineville Rd. (1332).
- 44.3 Left onto Buffalo Shoals Rd. (1004).
- 46.0 Left onto Kale Rd. (1832).
- 47.2 Right onto Long Island Rd. (1833).
- 48.1 Left onto Monbo Rd. (1885).
- 49.4 Right onto Molly's Backbone Rd. (1835).
- 52.1 Left onto Sherrills Ford Rd. (1848).
- 54.5 Right onto Slanting Bridge Rd. (1844).
- 60.8 The finish back in downtown Denver.

24

Alleghany
Back Roads Cruise

Doughton Park—Sparta
Laurel Springs—Doughton Park

This loop begins and ends at Doughton Park on the scenic Blue Ridge Parkway. The parkway's excellent landscape architecture often has a picture-postcard quality that glosses over daily existence in this region. Excursions just off the Blue Ridge offer a glimpse of the local culture.

The route passes through Alleghany County—the most sparsely populated county in North Carolina. Sparta, the county seat, marks the midway point in the loop. Sparta has that Mayberry atmosphere. Cruising down Main Street you might half expect to see Andy Griffith strolling down the sidewalk. In fact, the fictional town of Mayberry was modeled on Mount Airy, 30 miles to the east.

There are several thrilling descents and a few steep climbs along this route. For much of the journey, the road is surrounded by wildflowers and grassy cow pastures. A warm, sunny day in late spring or summer is the ideal time for this tour. You'll pass by Dr. Graybow's, home of the smoke-cured pipe, on your way into the town of Sparta. From Sparta, Hwy. 18 parallels a mountain stream as it winds back to the parkway. Numerous Christmas tree farms of fraser fir and blue spruce climb the hillsides. The Blue Ridge Parkway intersects Hwy. 18 at Laurel Springs. Back on the parkway you will have a brief reprieve of level cycling before the spectacular climb back to Doughton Park. The memorable views and the numerous overlooks make this final, strenuous leg of the journey very rewarding.

Doughton Park has constant reminders of the simple existence of the people of Appalachia. Split-rail fences line either side of the parkway, framing the rugged hillsides to either side. Brinegar and Caudill cabins remind us of the isolation early settlers experienced. A moonshine still remains behind Bluff Lodge. The challenging climb around Bluff Mountain and the speedy descent away from Doughton Park involve a bicyclist in a way no car traveler can experience.

This loop is just 34 miles long, but the challenging terrain may require extra time. Plan a full afternoon for the tour.

The Basics

Start: Doughton Park, located from milepost 238.6 through 244.8 on the Blue Ridge Parkway, has several parking areas. Bluff Lodge and Coffee Shop (milepost 241.1) has ample parking.
Length: 34.3 miles.
Terrain: Rolling hills with several fast descents and a few steep climbs. There is one extended climb from Laurel Springs back to Bluff Lodge in Doughton Park.
Food: Sparta around mile 12.5 has several fast-food restaurants. Laurel Springs at 27.0 has an amusing collection of tourist attractions including a restaurant and a small store. Bluff Lodge and Coffee Shop serves breakfast, lunch, and dinner.

Miles & Directions

- 0.0 From the coffee shop at Bluffs Lodge, ride north on the Blue Ridge Parkway. You will have a fast descent for much of the 7 miles on the parkway.
- 7.0 Left onto CR-1115. You will make a quick descent down this road. Use caution, and watch out for gravel. Follow the

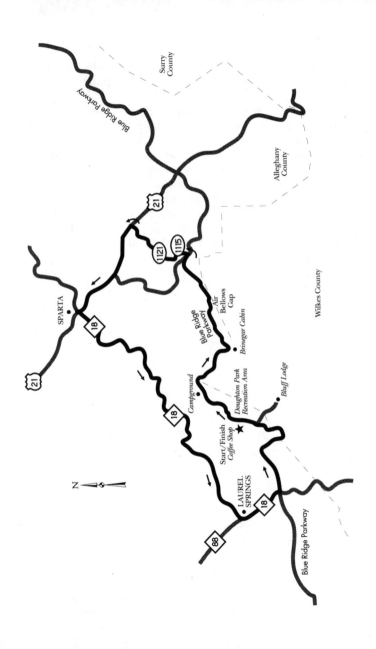

paved road, which winds past several farms into the valley. At mile 3 you will have a steep climb up to a stop sign.

- 10.4 Turn right onto CR-1121.
- 10.7 Turn left onto Hwy. 21 North. This two-lane highway into Sparta is well traveled. There is no shoulder, so be careful. Sparta is 1.7 miles ahead.
- 12.8 Turn left onto Hwy. 18 South (you are now in the center of downtown Sparta). Hwy. 18 quickly leaves any urban congestion to wander through the pleasantly rolling hills.
- 27.0 Enter Laurel Springs. Continue south on Hwy. 18.
- 27.3 On the far side of Laurel Springs, turn left onto the parkway, heading north once again. Enjoy the straightaway for the next few miles before the extended climb into the southern end of Doughton Park.
- 34.3 The parkway begins to level out as you approach Bluff Lodge and Coffee Shop.

25

Little Switzerland Ramble

Museum of North Carolina Minerals
Little Switzerland

Those of you eager to sample cycling in the Blue Ridge will find that the Little Switzerland Ramble offers many highlights of cycling over mountainous terrain in a mere 6½-mile loop. This ride includes an exhilarating descent on the Blue Ridge Parkway, a quick shoot through Little Switzerland Tunnel, back roads that hug the ridge line, scenic views of the Piedmont to the east, a visit to the village of Little Switzerland, and a taste of uphill cycling that will test your stamina.

This ride is simple and flexible. If you happen to be staying in Little Switzerland, you can begin the tour from your motel doorstep. If you're traveling through the area, you might begin the loop at the Museum of North Carolina Minerals in order to tackle the uphill climbs in the first half of the ride, have lunch and explore Little Switzerland in the middle, and finish off your ride with a downhill run along the Blue Ridge Parkway.

Keeping track of mileage is negligible in such a short ride. Simply follow the map, and take care at each turning point. The loop involves a mere two roads, the Blue Ridge Parkway and Highway 226A. The Blue Ridge Parkway is ideal for cycling, with its 45-mile-per-hour speed limit and lack of commercial truck traffic. Highway 226A has very little traffic, and cars generally travel in a cautious manner because of its winding character. Highway 226A does have a few blind curves, so use caution.

Little Switzerland is a festive area. The motels and lodges here have borrowed on the alpine theme, with motels and village shops built in the chalet style. Be sure to explore both clusters of the village, the Switzerland Inn complex and the village proper of Little Switzerland.

The Museum of North Carolina Minerals is an important destination no matter where you begin the loop. The National Park Service has constructed informative displays explaining the geology of the area. It is easy to see why rock hounds gravitate here. In fact, there are several active gem mines in the Little Switzerland/Spruce Pine area.

If you enjoy the Little Switzerland Ramble, keep in mind that the Blue Ridge Parkway lies before you with unlimited cycling possibilities.

The Basics

Start: You may begin this loop at the post office in the village of Little Switzerland or at the Museum of North Carolina Minerals, just outside the village. Parking can be found in both areas.
Length: 6.3 miles.
Terrain: Mountainous with a fast descent on the Blue Ridge Parkway and gradual climbs on Hwy. 226A. Low traffic except during peak tourist times, primarily during the month of October.
Food: The Switzerland Inn and the Switzerland Cafe both serve breakfast and lunch. They are in the village of Little Switzerland, which is either the starting point or midway point of this ride.

Miles & Directions

From the post office in Little Switzerland—

- 0.0 Follow Hwy. 226A toward the Blue Ridge Parkway.
- 0.1 Left at the jag connecting to the parkway (follow parkway signs).

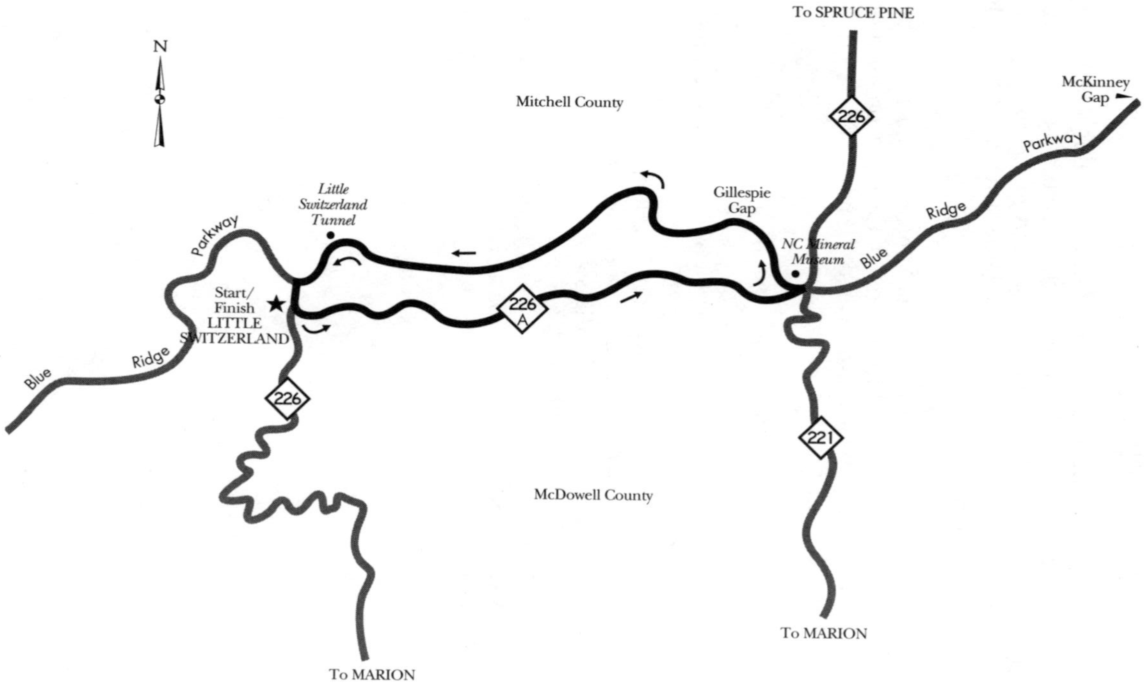
To SPRUCE PINE
N
Mitchell County
McKinney
Gap
226
Parkway
Little
Switzerland
Tunnel
Gillespie
Gap
Ridge
Parkway
NC Mineral
Museum
Blue
Start/
Finish
LITTLE
SWITZERLAND
226
A
Blue
Ridge
226
221
McDowell County
To MARION
To MARION

- 0.2 Right onto the Blue Ridge Parkway heading north. Get ready to pass through Little Switzerland Tunnel—use caution. The National Park Service *requires bicyclists to use front and rear lights* for visibility. At 542 feet long, Little Switzerland tunnel is among the shorter ones.
- 3.2 Exit left off the parkway.
- 3.3 The Museum of North Carolina Minerals is straight ahead. The loop continues left, at the bottom of the ramp, on Junction 226 South. Return to Little Switzerland on Hwy. 226A.
- 6.3 You are entering Little Switzerland.

From the Museum of North Carolina Minerals—

- 0.0 Proceed right from the parking lot on Hwy. 226A South toward Little Switzerland.
- 3.0 At the intersection of Hwy. 226, the loop heads right to connect with the Blue Ridge Parkway. Follow signs for the parkway. Note that the village of Little Switzerland is just a bit farther around the bend on Hwy. 226A.
- 3.2 Turn right onto the parkway heading north. Get ready for Little Switzerland Tunnel. Enjoy the descent on the parkway.
- 6.2 Get ready to exit left off the parkway; proceed down the exit ramp.
- 6.3 You're back at the museum parking lot.

26

Linville Gorge Classic

Linville Falls—Lake James
Table Rock—Linville Falls

For those who dare, the Linville Gorge Classic is a rugged, mountain bike challenge. This 50-mile loop follows U.S. Forest Service roads along the ridge line of the Linville Gorge Wilderness Area, a massive, 7,600-acre portion of Pisgah National Forest. The Linville River cuts a deep path through 3,000- and 4,000-foot mountains as it rushes in a 2,000-foot descent toward Lake James and the Piedmont.

The Forest Service roads winding through the Linville Gorge Wilderness Area are barely navigable for cyclists. Hard-packed gravel with deeply rutted portions, these roads have dramatically steep grades. You will break traction on the uphill climbs and go screaming down steep descents, snarling, "B-b-b-b-ba-a-d to the bone," in your grittiest, George Thorogood growl. Well, you'd better be. This ride will jar you—all the way to the bone.

Incredibly, the Linville Gorge was explored by bike well before the surge in mountain-bike popularity. Back in the seventies, the Appalachian State University Bicycle Club put together a small pamphlet of what are now classic bike rides in the Boone area. How club members cycled the Linville Gorge in prefat-tire days is a mystery. The roads have changed some since their *Bicycle Touring Guide to the Appalachian Mountain Region of North Carolina* was published. Forest Service Road 1261, for example, on the eastern side of the gorge, is entirely washed out and gated off now.

Twenty years hasn't changed the character of this ride, however.

The Appalachian State University Bicycle Club described the Linville Gorge Tour as "gruelling," advising that "the traveler of this route must possess endurance and a clear understanding of navigation in a deep wilderness area." Although the loop is only 49.5 miles in length, this is a sunup-to-sundown ride. Plan for every hazard you could possibly encounter. Have good rubber, bring basic tools, carry as much water as possible, and bring enough food for an entire day of strenuous effort. There are no, we repeat, *no stores* on the route. Bring a basic first-aid kit. It's wise also to carry a water-repellent jacket.

Don't go alone. We advise taking a friend on this ride. At the very least, tell someone your plans for the day. You will cycle briefly on two state highways (Highways 126 and 181) as you connect from one side of the gorge to the other. The route also travels through two housing developments. Otherwise, the majority of the route is within Linville Gorge Wilderness Area boundaries, which is entirely uninhabited forestland.

The Linville Gorge Classic makes an outstanding two-day ride. If you cut the ride in half, making the town of Linville Falls the midway point, you can start the ride at Rose Creek Campground in the valley and cycle up one side of the gorge the first day, descending the western side on the second day. (The campground owners will allow you to park overnight if you opt to stay over in Linville Falls.) Linville Falls also has several motels and restaurants. Hiking trails, near the gorge and Linville Falls, make pleasant diversions. We also include a short loop (option three), which we recommend for those tackling the gorge for the first time. It begins at Rose Creek Campground. This loop is tough enough with its extended climb up to Table Rock.

Any mountain-bike excursion involving the Linville Gorge is worth the effort. You will cycle through mixed hardwood forest with several varieties of birch, hickory, pine, oak, and maple trees. The stately Carolina hemlock is prevalent in the Linville Falls area. Hawksbill, Shortoff, and Long Arm are prominent mountains of the Linville area. The Forest Service roads are a minimal barrier to wildlife. White-tailed deer, woodchuck, raccoon, possum, black snake, and rattlesnake all inhabit the area. Red-tailed hawk soar above you. Blue aster, goldenrod, black-eyed Susan, oxeye daisy, bluet, and Queen Anne's lace are just a sampling of the wildflowers you can study during the slow, uphill climbs.

The complete Linville Gorge tour is for experienced cyclists only. Rudimentary knowledge of mountain-bike maneuvers is essential on the western side of the gorge. The Linville Gorge Classic receives notoriety as the most difficult ride of this book.

The Basics

Start: The Linville Gorge Wilderness Area/Linville Falls parking area is located 0.5 mile south on Hwy. 183 just beyond Linville Falls Community.

Length: 49.4 miles.

Terrain: Mountainous, gravel roads with severe grades and sharp, steep switchbacks. Mountain bikes only.

Food: Bring your own food and water—there are *absolutely no facilities* on this loop.

Special conditions: Bring basic tools, a first-aid kit, and a water-repellent jacket. This ride has more than its share of risk due to extreme road conditions and the possibility of sudden changes in weather.

For more information: Grandfather Ranger District, US-Forest Service, P.O. Box 519, Marion, NC 28752; (704) 652–2144.

Miles & Directions

- 0.0 The ride begins at the Linville Falls parking area. Signs on Hwy. 183 lead directly to parking area just outside the town of Linville Falls (CR-1238). Head toward the gorge on CR-1238, which is a gravel road.
- 3.8 Sign leading to Wisemans View. Continue straight.
- 15.6 Left onto NC-126, which is paved.
- 18.1 A one-lane bridge crosses the Linville River.
- 19.4 Lake James is to your right. There's a picnic area along the waterfront.

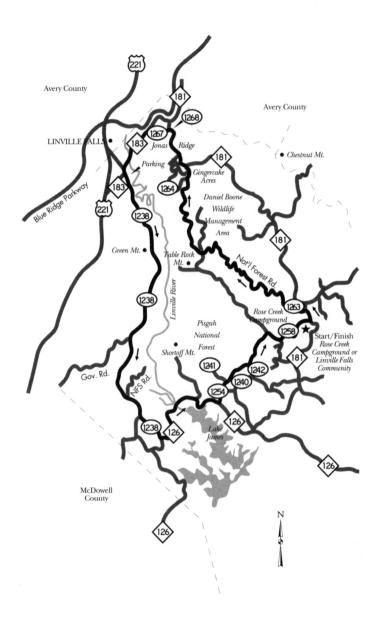

- 20.6 Left onto CR-1254.
- 23.7 Bear left. You will cross a one-lane bridge. Table Rock is visible to the left.
- 23.8 CR-1240 becomes paved by the fish hatchery.
- 24.9 CR-1261 intersects here. Keep going straight.
- 25.5 Left onto CR-1258 (gravel), which is also Rose Creek Rd. You will pass the Rose Creek Campground.
- 27.5 Left onto Hwy. 181 (paved).
- 28.0 Left onto CR-1263 (Simpson Creek Ave.). A U.S. Forest Service sign announces Table Rock.
- 28.3 Turn right at the sign for Table Rock Picnic Area. The road will now climb steadily toward Table Rock, with a few brief downhill switchbacks providing relief from the strenuous climb.
- 37.4 Table Rock Picnic Area is on the left. Continue straight. Brace yourself for steeper uphills as you climb between 3,500 and 4,000 feet.
- 41.9 Just when you thought you were lost in the wilderness, you enter a housing development called Gingercake Acres.
- 42.0 The road becomes paved and heads *downhill*. Whew!
- 42.9 At the fork, go straight.
- 43.2 Left onto Hwy. 181 North.
- 45.3 Left onto CR-1268 (Buckeye Hollow Rd.) in the community of Jonas Ridge.
- 45.5 Left onto CR-1267 (gravel). This is mostly downhill.
- 47.2 Left onto Hwy. 183 (paved). You've got a downhill stretch back to the Linville Falls parking area.
- 49.2 Left into the Linville Falls parking area.
- 49.4 At last, you've made a full circle around the gorge.

For an overnight, two-day option—

To divide this tour into two days, begin at mile 25.5, at the Rose Creek Campground. The proprietors of the campground will allow you to park your vehicle overnight. Begin your tour with the second half of the loop up the eastern side of the gorge. This divides the ride in half with an overnight stay in Linville Falls. (Be sure to make reservations for lodging in Linville Falls. There are also numerous campsites along the forest service road on the western side of the gorge.) Remember, the eastern side of the gorge sustains the most strenuous climbs, while the western side is notable for its tricky, technical descents. This makes Day 1 24.0 miles; Day 2 is 25.4 miles.

For the Table Rock Challenge option—

This option combines the best elements of mountain biking the gorge with a little less effort. The full loop around the gorge really is extreme, so if you are the least bit tentative, try this first. Begin at Rose Creek Campground. Follow directions beginning at mile 25.5. The first half of this loop is one long hill climb with views of Table Rock challenging you along. It's tough, indeed. The second half of the loop, however, is all reward. Instead of turning left on Hwy. 81 toward Linville Falls, you turn right for an exhilarating descent on paved roads back to Rose Creek Campground. The ascent will take you two to three hours, but you'll complete your descent in less than an hour.

27

Grandfather Mountain Cruise

Blue Ridge Parkway

Grandfather Mountain may be the most recognizable peak in western North Carolina. If its broad base and jagged slopes were not enough, the Highland Games and Gathering of the Scottish Clans, the "Mile-High Swinging Bridge," and Mildred the Bear have helped make the mountain legendary.

The Grandfather Mountain Cruise is a thrill-a-minute bicycle loop. In 18 miles you wind around switchbacks on a segment of the mountain's base on Highway 221, then ascend the mountain's side on the Blue Ridge Parkway. In the final miles of the loop, you cross the Linn Cove Viaduct, the engineering masterpiece that completed the Blue Ridge Parkway in 1989. Before the completion of the viaduct, Highway 221 was the official parkway detour around the mountain. Highway 221 remains memorable not only for its beauty, but for the farmers that sell their apple cider, apple butter, apples, honey, and molasses at roadside stands.

Cycling along Highway 221 is like shooting through a vast rock garden of massive boulders, waterfalls, hemlock, and rhododendron. As you maneuver the curves, your eyes catch side-glances of primeval forest. Grandfather is cool, damp, and craggy with mossy nooks and crannies. It's a sometimes forbidding place for a bicyclist, where fog and rain can set in for days and winds can whip through with awesome power.

Cyclists are drawn to Grandfather's challenges. Once a year Grandfather Mountain opens its park doors to hundreds of cyclists who attempt the Bridge-to-Bridge century that climbs the park road to the summit. Grandfather crests at 5,938 feet at Galloway Peak. In this loop the elevations along the Blue Ridge Parkway range between 3,500 feet and 4,300 feet.

Although the climb is steady along the parkway, this loop is easy relative to its rewards. You can choose your pain and pleasure by where you begin this ride and in which direction you choose to cycle. The parkway segment is downhill heading north, a steady uphill going south. Highway 221 is also primarily downhill heading north and uphill heading south. The Grandfather Mountain Cruise is one of the best routes around for experiencing a single mountain by bicycle.

The Basics

Start: The loop begins at the Beacon Heights Overlook at milepost 305.2 on the Blue Ridge Parkway. You should find ample parking here.

Length: 18.3 miles.

Terrain: Rolling to mountainous. Hwy. 221, with its quick descents on sharp curves, requires competent bike-handling skills. The segment along the parkway is a gradual climb to the Linn Cove Viaduct.

Food: There are two country stores midway (mile 9.6) at the intersection of Hwy. 221 and Holloway Mt. Rd. (one store is on Holloway Mt. Rd.).

Miles & Directions

- 0.0 Head north on the Blue Ridge Parkway from the Beacon Heights Overlook.
- 0.2 Left at exit off the parkway onto Hwy. 221.
- 0.3 Left heading north on Hwy. 221 toward Blowing Rock. Get ready to rock and roll!

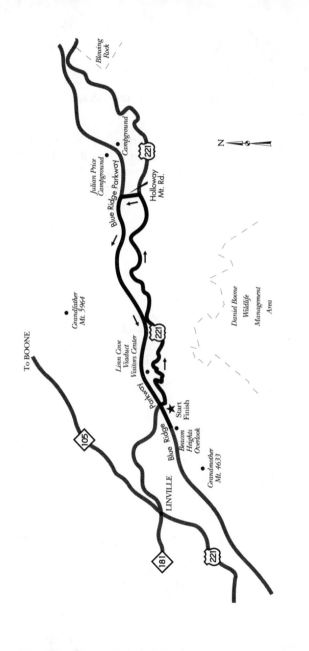

- 3.6 A state roadside park is on your right, with picnic area, water, and rest rooms.
- 7.9 Boone Fork parking area with trail access to Grandfather Mountain.
- 9.6 Turn left onto Holloway Mt. Road.
- 10.6 Turn right onto ramp to enter the Blue Ridge Parkway.
- 10.7 Turn left (heading south) onto the Blue Ridge Parkway.
- 17.3 Linn Cove Viaduct Visitors Center on left.
- 18.3 Beacon Heights Overlook.

South Carolina

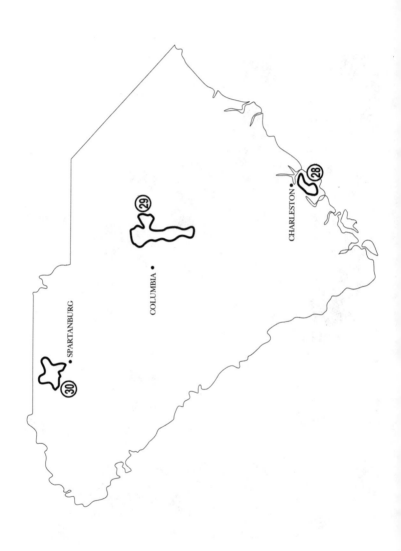

SPARTANBURG

COLUMBIA

CHARLESTON

㉘

㉙

㉚

South Carolina

28

Carolina Low Country Challenge

Folly Beach—Oak Island—James Island
Johns Island—Wadmalaw Island—Rockville
Wadmalaw Island—Johns Island
James Island—Oak Island—Folly Beach

This ride, adapted from the Coastal Cyclists' Fall Century, travels through the Low Country south of the historic Charleston peninsula. The route hops from island to island past tall palmettos, sprawling live oak canopies and salt marsh lining the Intracoastal Waterway. In the cool, sea breeze of a spring or fall day, this ride is a pleasurable way to break up an intense tour of Charleston.

Water dominates the physical geography of the area. In a single bike ride, you will cycle from the Atlantic Ocean to the Intracoastal Waterway crossing every type of waterway in between. The Folly River, Oak Island Creek, Long Island River, the Stono River, and Church Creek are all crossed by bridge. The Intracoastal Waterway is an important thoroughfare throughout the South. A stroll through one of the many marinas in Charleston will find yachts and sailboats from cities as far south as Savannah, Jacksonville, and Miami and points north including Wilmington, Norfolk, and Baltimore.

Although developers are creeping out to the islands surrounding Charleston, the route is much less developed than one might expect given its proximity to the city. A trip down canopied River Road on Johns Island is accompanied by moderate traffic in a residential area of medium-to-large estates.

Wadmalaw Island manages to hold development to a minimum. While a handful of stately homes commands views of the Intracoastal Waterway, the island is wild enough to warrant an occasional group of hunters. Truck crops, such as the tomatoes grown by Sunny Point Tomatoes, keep considerable acreage under cultivation. The American Tea Company, also on Wadmalaw, is the only grower and harvester of tea in the continental United States. Short, bushy tea plants can be seen on the way to the fishing village of Rockville.

The full 74-mile route turns around at the Cherry Point boat landing on the Intracoastal Waterway. Cherry Point is a good place to "set a spell" before heading back to Folly Beach. A picnic area shaded by live oaks invites you to breathe deep the briny smells of the fishing trade. You can cycle all the way back to the Atlantic contemplating your favorite seafood delight.

Hidden less than a half mile from the bike route on Johns Island sits Angel Oak *(Quercus virginiana),* a fourteen-hundred-year-old live oak tree said to be the oldest living thing east of the Mississippi. Plan for a side trip to the site either on the way or the way back from Wadmalaw Island—it's a mere 0.3-mile detour. Contemplating the soul of this ancient tree with limbs spanning more than 160 feet is worth pushing your bike tires through sand and dirt. The City of Charleston operates a picnic area with a gift shop that sells snacks and live oak memorabilia.

As you pedal closer to the Atlantic Ocean, you may encounter increasing head winds resulting from sea breezes off the ocean. On most of the route, you should encounter cross winds, but the final 4 miles can be dead into the wind.

Folly Beach brings back romantic summer memories for many, although Hurricane Hugo literally swept away monuments to this history. The Folly Beach Pavilion was central to this nostalgia as a mecca for dancing spanning the big band era of the thirties and forties and the "Shag" and beach music of the sixties. Not a trace of the pavilion remains where the Holiday Inn now stands.

Although the Folly Beach Pavilion was torn down well before Hurricane Hugo, the 1989 hurricane eroded much of the beachfront north and south of Charleston. This is dramatically evident in Folly Beach's total lack of sand and beachfront. The Holiday Inn backs right into the ocean, with a sea wall and large rocks desperately holding the ocean at bay.

The Carolina Low Country Challenge is reason enough to visit the Charleston area. If you've been looking for an excuse to visit Charleston, why not sign up for the Coastal Cyclists' spring or fall century ride? Mountain bikes are an outstanding mode of transportation, incidentally, for exploring Charleston's city streets. Bumpy cobblestone thoroughfares and narrow alleyways provide hours of exploration. Bikes allow the perfect pace for gazing at the pastel, brick, and granite homes of Charleston. (Be sure to bring a bike lock so you can explore interiors without worrying about the security of your bike.) Plan for at least three days to explore the area.

The Basics

Start: Park in Folly Beach. The ride begins in front of the Folly Beach Holiday Inn.
Length: 61.8 or 73.6 miles.
Terrain: Flat.
Food: There are convenience stores at 11.8, 27.3, and 56.4 miles. You may want to stop for lunch along Bohicket Rd. at miles 26.8 and 56.5 coming and going. If you can wait until the end, try Cappy's Seafood at 63.5.
For more information: Larry Whetsell, Coastal Cyclists, 120 Southwold Circle, Goose Creek, SC 29445; (803) 553–5283.

Miles & Directions

For the 73.6-mile option—

- 0.0   From the Holiday Inn proceed on Center St.
- 3.6   Left onto Grimball Rd.

- 5.3 Sharp left onto Riverland Dr. at powerhouse.
- 7.6 Entrance to James Island County Park (camping and recreation).
- 9.2 Left onto Maybank Hwy. at light.
- 9.9 Cross the Stono River. **Caution: metal grate bridge.**
- 11.8 Right onto River Rd. at light.
- 16.5 Cross Main, and continue straight onto Chisolm Rd.
- 22.7 Follow Chisolm as it turns sharply to the left.
- 24.1 Follow Chisolm as it turns sharply to the right.
- 24.4 Continue straight on Chisolm.
- 26.3 Right onto Main at St. John's High School (Bohicket Rd.).
- 27.3 Right onto Maybank Hwy. at light. **Caution: heavy traffic on Maybank Hwy.**

- *27.6 Left onto Angel Oak Rd. (St. Johns Episcopal Church is on the corner.) Proceed 0.3 mile down a dirt road to Angel Oak Park, site of Angel Oak. The park is open daily 9:00 A.M. to 5:00 P.M.*

- 28.0 Cross Church Creek onto Wadmalaw Island.
- 30.1 Veer right at Y onto Bear Bluff Rd.
- 33.6 Right onto Harts Bluff Rd.
- 36.4 Cross Bear Bluff Rd., and continue onto Liberia.
- 38.1 Right onto Maybank Hwy. at T intersection.
- 43.1 U-turn at dead end in Rockville.
- 43.5 Right onto Cherry Point Rd.
- 44.5 U-turn at Cherry Point Boat Landing.
- 45.5 Right onto Maybank Hwy.
- 55.7 Cross Church Creek.
- 56.4 Left onto Bohicket Rd. at light.
- 56.7 Right onto Brownswood Rd.
- 60.3 Right onto River Rd. at T intersection.
- 62.8 Left onto Maybank Hwy. at light.
- 63.5 Cross Stono River.
- 64.4 Right onto Riverland Dr.
- 68.3 Sharp right onto Grimball Rd. at stop sign.
- 70.0 Right onto Folly Rd. at stop sign.
- 73.6 End at the Holiday Inn in Folly Beach.

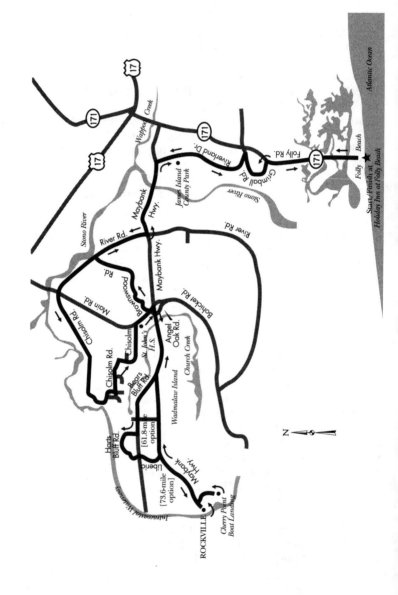

17 · 171 · 171 · 17

Wappoo Creek

Stono River

Maybank Hwy.

River Rd.

171

Riverland Dr.

Grimball Rd.

James Island County Park

Folly Rd.

171

Folly Beach

Atlantic Ocean

Start/Finish at Holiday Inn at Folly Beach

Brownswood Rd.

Main Rd.

Chisolm Rd.

Chisolm Rd.

Chisolm

Bears Bluff Rd.

Harts Bluff Rd.

[61.8-mile option]

Liberia

Maybank Hwy.

[73.6-mile option]

ROCKVILLE

Cherry Point Boat Landing

Intracoastal Waterway

Wadmalaw Island

St. John's H.S.

Angel Oak Rd.

Church Creek

Bohicket Rd.

River Rd.

Maybank Hwy.

Stono River

N

For the 61.8-mile option, follow directions above through 36.4 miles, and then—

- 38.1 Left onto Maybank Hwy.
- 44.6 Left onto Bohicket Rd. at light.
- 44.9 Right onto Brownswood Rd.
- 48.5 Right onto River Rd. at T intersection.
- 51.0 Left onto Maybank Hwy. at light.
- 51.7 Cross the Stono River.
- 52.6 Right onto Riverland Dr.
- 56.5 Sharp right onto Grimball Rd. at stop sign.
- 58.2 Right onto Folly Rd. at stop sign.
- 61.8 End at the Holiday Inn at Folly Beach.

29

Sumter "Lizard Man" Classic

Sumter—Pack's Landing—Sumter
Rembert—Sumter

Reporters for CNN, *Omni Magazine,* and *Time* have all visited the Sumter area to check out the freaky phenomenon. So, heck, thought members of the Sumter Chain Gang Bicycle Club, why don't we name a bike ride after the scaly, green creature? We'll send a pack of maniac cyclists out to scour the back roads of Lee, Clarendon, and Sumter counties in search of Lizard Man. No matter that Lizard Man's glow-in-the-dark, red eyes shun harsh sunlight. If he's out there, cyclists will surely find him.

So, on a sizzling September morning one hundred cyclists added a new dimension to their Sunday bike ride. It was eighty degrees when the ride began, and the South Carolina heat kept getting hotter and hotter. "We're experiencing a Bermuda high," the weatherman said. Ninety-five degrees and there's no shade.

Lizard Man, a mythical creature first sighted in 1988, is said to reside in Scape Ore Swamp in Lee County. He has been sighted on several different occasions by area residents passing by the swamp. While the bicycle route does not venture into Scape Ore Swamp, it does pass by many swampy areas.

The metric century route (62.3 miles) heads out from Shaw Air Force Base in a southerly direction. The terrain surrounding Sumter is fairly flat, with the occasional steep hill providing an unexpected challenge. The beginning miles make an inspiring sweep past the Shaw AFB runway.

If you're lucky, you might see an F-16 or an OV-10 take off or land. Shaw Air Force Base is home to the 363rd Tactical Fighter Wing and the 507th Tactical Air Control Wing. Shaw's F-16 unit was the first of its type to reach the Persian Gulf in the 1991 conflict. Battens Store at mile 50 on the metric route proudly displays photographs and memorabilia from the Persian Gulf beneath its glass countertop.

You may notice hurricane evacuation signs along the route. The devastating force of Hurricane Hugo is still remembered vividly by Sumter residents. If you look closely at the rows of loblolly pine, you may see that they are not all straight and perfect. Hugo uprooted many trees as it traveled inland from Charleston, South Carolina, to Charlotte, North Carolina, and as far inland as the Blue Ridge Parkway. The countryside alternates from corn, cotton, and soybean fields to perfectly straight rows of loblolly pine trees.

The metric century makes its midway point at Pack's Landing along Lake Marion. The marina makes a good place for a snack before heading back toward Sumter. If you choose to cycle a full century (100 miles), the route will double back to Shaw AFB Youth Center before completing a figure eight by following a northern loop for the remaining 38.8 miles.

North of Sumter the terrain gets a bit hillier. Grassy horse farms break up the monotony of the nondescript pine barrens that occur naturally in the area. If you need a break, the town of Rembert has a county store.

The metric loop passes by Poinsett State Park at mile 44 along Highway 261. Located on the edge of Wateree Swamp, the park is a popular overnight cycling destination for Columbia, South Carolina, cyclists. It would make an excellent base camp for cycling the metric century.

While the scenery along the Sumter Lizard Man Classic is not spectacular, all that local drama sure can fire the imagination. After cycling the Lizard Man Lair Century, we can understand how sightings of Lizard Man might occur. The Sumter bicycle club didn't dub themselves the "Chain Gang" without good reason. The South

Carolina heat can be relentless. If you do not relish suffering, you might choose a day when temperatures are forecast no higher than the low eighties.

Even then, you may never sight Lizard Man. He is undoubtedly smarter than most bicyclists, preferring the cool recesses of Scape Ore Swamp to the heat of the South Carolina back roads.

The Basics

Start: The ride begins at Shaw Air Force Base Youth Center in Sumter, S.C. From Columbia, S.C., on US-378, turn left onto SC-441 just before Shaw AFB. Continue past the back gate at Shaw to the traffic light, and turn right. The youth center is the first large building on the right. Turn on the first street. Approaching from the east on US-378 from Sumter, drive past the main entrance to Shaw to intersection of SC-441, and turn right. Follow above directions from here.

Length: 38.8, 62.3, or 101.1 miles.

Terrain: Flat to hilly.

Food: There are several country stores along the route. You will find stores at Pack's Landing (32.4 miles) and Batten Store (49.3) on the metric route and in the town of Rembert (26.6) on the 38-mile route.

For more information: Buddy's Schwinn, 45 Wesmark Blvd., Sumter, SC 29150; (803) 773-8134.

Miles & Directions

For the 62.3-mile option—

- 0.0 Proceed left out the gate of the Shaw AFB Youth Center.
- 0.2 Bear right, then left onto Hwy. 441.
- 2.4 Left onto SC-378. Use caution at this intersection. Hwy. 378 is a major four-lane highway (it has a paved shoulder).
- 3.8 Right onto Eagle Rd. (by Roxy's).

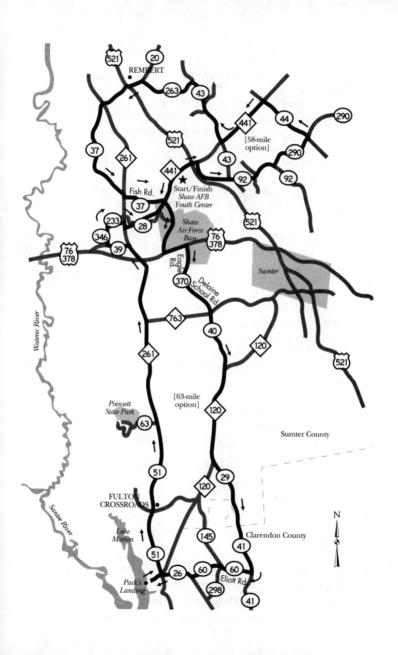

- 5.1 **Caution: railroad crossing.**
- 5.8 Left onto SC-370 (Delaine School Rd.).
- 8.6 Cross railroad tracks.
- 12.4 Yield onto SC-120.
- 17.6 Left at the second Y intersection onto SC-29.
- 18.0 Railroad crossing.
- 22.3 Clarendon County line. SC-29 becomes SC-41.
- 25.2 Right onto SC-60 (Elliott Rd.).
- 27.1 Yield left, staying on SC-60. Watch for gravel.
- 29.6 Right onto SC-26 (Gov. Richardson Rd.).
- 31.3 County line. Railroad crossing.
- 31.4 Left following signs to Pack's Landing. (This was a rest stop on the Lizard Man Lair Century; it's a 1-mile detour out and back.)
- 32.4 Pack's Landing. View of Lake Marion. From Pack's Landing head back to SC-51.
- 33.4 Left onto SC-51.
- 40.5 Left onto SC-261.
- 44.0 Poinsett State Park.
- 49.3 Railroad crossing.
- 53.2 **Use extreme caution crossing SC-378 at the blinking yellow light.**
- 54.3 Left onto SC-39.
- 55.4 Railroad crossing.
- 55.5 Right onto SC-346.
- 56.6 Right onto SC-233. Railroad crossing.
- 57.7 Right onto SC-261.
- 58.1 Left onto SC-28.
- 60.0 Right onto Fish Rd.
- 61.3 Left onto Hwy. 441.
- 62.3 End at youth center.

For the 38.8-mile option—

- 0.0 Begin at Shaw AFB Youth Center. Turn right at the gate. Right onto Hwy. 441 (Frierson Rd.).
- 3.7 Cross US-521 at the caution light.

- 4.1 Right onto Old US-521.
- 5.0 Yield left onto SC-92 (Queens Chapel Rd.) by Rabon's Sav-on. Watch for gravel.
- 7.9 Left onto SC-290 (Westbury Mill Rd.).
- 8.8 Bear right on curve.
- 10.8 Left onto SC-44. Dubose Siding.
- 14.4 Left onto Hwy. 441. Watch for loose gravel.
- 18.0 Right onto SC-43 (Black River Rd.) Watch for sand.
- 22.1 Left onto SC-263 (New Hope Church Rd.).
- 24.1 Look out for **dogs** at the house at the bottom of the hill.
- 25.8 Left onto SC-20.
- 26.6 Right onto SC-521. Entering the town of Rembert.
- 26.8 Left onto SC-37.
- 32.7 Bear left, staying on SC-37.
- 33.2 Railroad crossing.
- 34.6 Right onto SC-261.
- 35.1 Left onto SC-37 (Fish Rd.).
- 37.6 Right onto Hwy. 441.
- 38.8 End at youth center.

For the 101.1-mile option, simply complete both of the above routes.

30

The Spartanburg Challenge

Spartanburg—Boiling Springs
Cherokee Springs—Spartanburg

The Spartanburg Freewheelers are known throughout the southeast as the bicycle club behind the annual Assault on Mt. Mitchell. Drawing sixteen-hundred participants along with their families and friends, this 102-mile ascent to the top of Mt. Mitchell has become an event of national stature. The Spartanburg Freewheelers have developed an equally successful event in their annual Spartan Century Circuit. Not nearly as big in terms of participants, the Spartan Century Circuit is a pleasant tour through the peach groves and watermelon fields of northern South Carolina.

The Spartanburg Challenge features two 50-mile loops from the Spartan Century Circuit. These loops can be cycled individually or joined together in a figure eight to make a century (100 miles). The countryside north of Spartanburg rises gradually to meet the Blue Ridge Mountains. Properly known as foothills, their rolling to hilly terrain has elevations ranging from 500 to 1,000 feet.

Rambling through peach groves as it does, the Spartanburg Challenge makes an outstanding spring tour. The peach blossoms put forth a fragrant tour de force between mid-March and mid-April depending upon the severity of the preceding winter. If you're traveling to Spartanburg via I–85 north from Charlotte, you'll have no doubt you are in the heart of "peach country" when you see the massive Gaultney peach standing in all its sensual glory.

Then again, if you time your tour around the peach harvest, between the summer months of June and August, you can fuel the entire ride on that singularly delectable, truly southern fruit. Although peaches are long gone by October, you should find the leaves in varying stages of change as you gaze toward the Blue Ridge.

There is no ultimate destination on this ride. The enjoyment lies in the ride itself as you savor the beauty of the countryside. Occasionally, kudzu takes over in places where the land has no immediate interest for man. Morning glories in fuchsia, white, and magenta are a special treat for early risers. For the most part, farms parcel the hillsides into pasture, peach groves, garden plots, fields for corn, beans, and watermelon.

By and large, the simple, white clapboard churches you'll pass at nearly every crossroad are the dominant community structures: Cooley Springs Church, Rainbow Church, Alversons Grove Church, Brookland Church, Buck Creek Church, North Pecolet Church, and on and on with as many congregations as there are family roots or landmarks to name them by.

The Spartanburg Challenge can be undertaken as an intense, masterful workout on hilly terrain; or it can be savored as an all-day ramble of the countryside. Either way, it's sure to please.

The Basics

Start: Begin at the University of South Carolina at Spartanburg (USCS). Visitor parking is available. There are signs and exits on I–85 and I–26.

Length: 49.0, 50.6, and 100.0 miles.

Terrain: Rolling to hilly.

Food: There are several stores along the way in Boiling Springs and at smaller unnamed crossroads. Look for convenience stores at 8.1 and 26.8 miles on the first loop and at 2.1, 31.6, and 44.2 on the second loop. Be sure to carry plenty of fluids.

For more information: Spartanburg Chapter, American Diabetes Association, P.O. Box 8285, Spartanburg, SC 29305.

Miles & Directions

The following two 50-mile loops can be cycled separately or combined to make a century.

For the 50.6-mile option (this is the route cycled first on the Spartan Century Circuit)—

- 0.0 Leave the Hodge Center on the USCS campus.
- 0.1 Right onto University Way.
- 0.6 Right onto Valley Falls Rd.
- 2.0 Left onto Hanging Rock Rd. (just after bridge).
- 4.5 Right onto Old Furnace Rd.
- 5.7 Straight ahead. Traffic light here. Cross Hwy. 9.
- 11.2 Left onto Peachtree Rd.
- 12.2 Cross bridge over the Pacolet River. **Caution: There are several bumps and gaps on the bridge.**
- 15.1 Straight. **Stop** at the intersection with SC-11. This is the N.C. border.
- 20.7 Right onto Green Creek Rd.
- 23.8 Rutherford County line.
- 26.8 Providence Weslyan Church.
- 28.5 Straight. Use caution crossing SC-11.
- 31.6 Left onto Buck Creek Rd. (note Cy Turner Exterminator).
- 34.6 Right onto Casey Creek Rd. at Buck Creek Church.
- 34.9 Cross Lake Blalock.
- 38.4 Right onto Cherokee Circle.
- 38.5 Right onto Old Furnace Rd.
- 40.6 Right onto Foster's Grove Rd.
- 41.6 Left onto Overcreek Rd.
- 43.2 Left onto Parris Bridge Rd.
- 48.2 Left at traffic light onto SC-9. **Use caution making this left turn.**
- 48.3 Immediate right onto Old Boiling Springs Rd.; Old Boiling Springs Rd. bears left.
- 49.2 Right onto University Way/Milliken Way.
- 50.2 Right onto University Way and I–85 off ramp (confusing

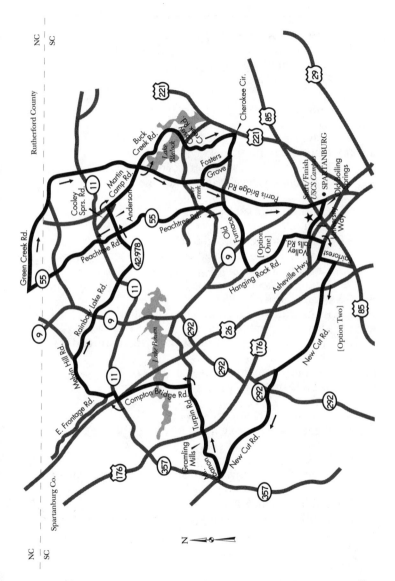

here). USCS is just ahead.

- 50.3 Right onto University Way (parallels US-176).
- 50.5 Right onto Hodge Rd.
- 50.6 Finish at Hodge Center (USCS).

For the 49-mile option—

- 0.0 Leave Hodge Center on the USCS campus.
- 0.1 Right onto University Way.
- 0.6 Left onto Valley Falls Rd. (cross over US-176).
- 1.3 Right onto Asheville Hwy. (four-lane).
- 2.1 Left onto Fairforest Rd.
- 2.5 **Caution: railroad tracks.**
- 3.0 Right onto New Cut.
- 4.0 **Caution: more railroad tracks.**
- 4.4 Straight. Proceed through traffic light, crossing I–26.
- 6.7 Straight. Note Foothills Tack Shop.
- 9.3 Left fork toward Gowansville.
- 10.3 Straight. Cross SC-292.
- 14.2 Right onto Mt. Lebanon Rd. to Gramling.
- 15.7 Right on Gramling Mills Rd.
- 16.9 Straight on Turpin Rd. Cross US-176 and **railroad tracks.**
- 17.5 Left onto SC-42-127.
- 19.4 Left onto Compton Bridge Rd. (SC-42-37).
- 21.3 Cross Lake Bowen.
- 23.4 Right onto Hwy. 11.
- 23.8 Left onto East Frontage Rd.
- 24.2 Right fork onto Melvin Hill Rd.
- 26.8 Right onto Rainbow Lake Rd. (SC-42-92).
- 29.5 Cross SC-9.
- 31.6 Cross SC-11 at Fingerville Baptist Church and Don's Quick Shop.
- 32.8 Left onto Anderson Rd. (SC-42-978).
- 32.9 **Caution: one-lane bridge.**
- 32.9 Left onto Anderson Rd.
- 34.5 Straight. Cross SC-42-55.
- 35.6 Right onto Cooley Springs Rd.

- 36.1 Right onto Martin Camp Rd.
- 38.2 Right onto Parris Bridge Rd. (SC-42).
- 40.9 Pass Mt. View Baptist Church on right.
- 43.0 Straight. Cross Old Furnace Rd. There's a blinking light near the water tower.
- 46.7 Left at red light onto SC-9 (four-lane).
- 46.8 Right onto Old Boiling Springs Rd.
- 46.8 Immediate left onto Old Boiling Springs Rd.
- 47.6 Right onto University Way/Milliken Way.
- 48.6 Right onto University Way and I–85 off ramp. **Use caution.**
- 48.7 Right onto University Way (parallels US-176).
- 48.9 Right onto Hodge Rd.
- 49.0 Finish at the Hodge Center on USCS campus.

Tennessee

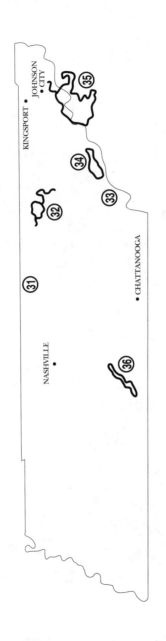

Tennessee

31

Big South Fork Ramble

Bandy Creek Campground
(Big South Fork National River and Recreation Area)

The mountain-bike rambles featured here are bound up in the vision of Joe Cross, president of the Big South Fork Bicycle Club of Oneida, Tennessee. Joe has worked as a volunteer consultant with the National Park Service in constructing several mountain-bike loops within the Big South Fork National River and Recreation Area. Joe urged us to visit this lesser-known, nearly new national park that he is fortunate to have right in his backyard.

Ever heard of the Big South Fork? If you're into running white water, you have. Most of the major outfitters in the Southeast offer guided trips on the Big South Fork of the Cumberland River. Rapids with names like the Ell, Jake's Hole, the Washing Machine, and O & W Rapid lure thrill seekers to the park.

While the river is well known, the park and its facilities may not be. If mountain biking is your passion, you will definitely want to spend a full weekend in the park. The park lies along the Cumberland Plateau in northeastern Tennessee and southeastern Kentucky. The Cumberland Plateau is a spur of the Appalachian Mountains spanning as far north as West Virginia and south as far as Birmingham, Alabama. Elevations level out into a tableland in the 1,500- to 2,000-foot range.

The rides featured here begin at Bandy Creek Campground, which is located about halfway between Oneida, Tennessee, and

Jamestown, Tennessee. Roughly 12 miles of trails are designated specifically for mountain-bike use. These trails hook up with a network of equestrian trails. Mountain bikes are allowed on the horse trails, adding many more miles for exploration. The developed trails range in length from Duncan Hollow Loop at 5.3 miles to Collier Ridge Loop at 8.0 miles. The trails are flat to rolling through forested areas. Trail conditions range from single track paths designated for mountain bikes only to wider equestrian trails shared with horseback riders. Brief stretches follow gravel roads traveled by the occasional car.

Joe Cross is working currently with the park service to extend the mountain-bike trails beyond park boundaries to hook up with an abandoned O & W railroad bed that follows along the gorge overlooking the Big South Fork.

To visit the park, you really should have several days for exploration in the area. The history of this Tennessee–Kentucky region is a fascinating story of human toil dominated by one natural resource. Rich deposits of bituminous coal supported a rigorous mining industry through much of the 1900s. Heavy mining threatened to destroy forests and streams until the National Park Service stepped in to preserve the area.

If you visit the Big South Fork, be sure to set aside half a day to explore the Blue Heron Mining community on the Kentucky side of the park. The park service has done an outstanding job depicting the difficulties of the mining life. Ghost structures recreate the mining community as it thrived under the ownership of the Stearns Coal and Lumber Company between 1937 and 1962. Historians have collected the oral histories of people who grew up at Blue Heron. You walk from the school house to the company store and across the Big South Fork River over a railroad trestle filled with the voices of men and women who grew up at Blue Heron. You feel their isolation and their frustrations.

The National Park Service and the U.S. Army Corps of Engineers have done a remarkable job on the physical layout and construction of the park facilities. Camping is quite luxurious with solar-powered bath houses providing electric lighting and hot showers. There's even a swimming pool, which is free to campers.

Spring and fall may be the best seasons to visit, but we think any season would be enjoyable. In addition to these mountain-bike rides, you may want to cycle the Cumberland Plateau Challenge that ends at Bandy Creek.

The Basics

Start: Both rides begin at Bandy Creek Campground Visitor Center. Bandy Creek Campground is about an hour's drive north of Knoxville. Take I–75 North to TN-63 West. Follow signs to Big South Fork National River and Recreation Area. If traveling from Nashville, take I–40 East and exit onto TN-27 North toward Oneida.
Length: 5.3 and 8.0 miles.
Terrain: Flat to rolling.
Food: There are plans for a camp store at Bandy Creek Campground. Right now there are only drink and snack machines at the visitor center.
For more information: Superintendent, Big South Fork National River and Recreation Area, P.O. Drawer 630, Oneida, TN 37841; (615) 879-4013.

Miles & Directions

Park rangers recommend checking in with the Bandy Creek Visitor Center for the latest developments on the mountain-bike trails. They will provide you with maps and up-to-date information on the conditions on the trails.

Duncan Hollow Loop

This trail is easy to moderate with a few puddles. The trail is marked with four-by-four-foot signs with orange letters and orange arrowheads about 1 foot off the ground at turns.

- 0.0 Trail begins at Bandy Creek Visitor Center. Leaving the visitor center, go across Bandy Creek Rd. toward the campground and swimming pool.
- 0.2 Turn left toward Area A. Near swimming pool look for the gravel road and four-by-four post indicating BIKE TRAIL. This is the Duncan Hollow Rd.
- 0.5 Sign on right indicates Scott State Forest.
- 0.7 Watch for horses entering on your left. Part of Duncan Hollow Rd. is shared by horses.
- 1.1 TVA power lines. Look for the four-by-four marker post on left.
- 1.5 Left turn off Duncan Hollow Road. Look for four-by-four marker post.
- 1.8 Begin downhill section.
- 2.0 Should be at the bottom of hill. Continue on the trail as it veers to the left. (On right is a closed road and a NO HORSE sign.)
- 2.1 Look for the four-by-four marker post. The main road turns left, but the bike trail is straight ahead. Should also see a NO HORSE sign.
- 2.5 Make a sharp, right turn, and begin a downhill section.
- 2.6 Small creek crossing. This can be difficult for beginning riders, but *all* riders are urged to be cautious on both the entrance and exit at the creek.
- 2.9 Veer to your left, and begin downhill section.
- 3.1 Trail gets very narrow at bottom of hill.
- 3.2 Right turn at top of hill.
- 3.8 Turn left to return to Bandy Creek Visitor Center. You can also turn right for another lap if desired.
- 3.9 Right turn onto Duncan Hollow Rd. Look for four-by-four marker.
- 5.3 End at visitor center.

Collier Ridge Loop Trail

This ride is moderately difficult. The trail is marked by white arrows on brown metal signs or orange arrows on wooden four-by-four-foot posts.

- 0.0 From Bandy Creek Visitor Center, turn left onto Bandy Creek Rd. (Don't go toward the stables or enter the campground. If you make the correct turn, the swimming pool is on the right.)
- 0.3 Pavement changes to gravel.
- 0.4 Horse trail crosses the gravel road. Stop for horses to pass.
- 0.9 Katie Blevins Cemetery on the right.
- 1.1 Scott State Forest sign on left. Bicycles exit left just beyond sign.
- 1.2 Hiking trail crosses the bicycle trail.
- 1.4 Cross North Bandy Creek. Hiking trail marked with red arrowhead blaze will join with the bike trail in less than 0.1 mile; stay left.
- 1.8 Cross King Branch.
- 2.0 Hiking trail goes left, bicycles straight ahead.
- 2.2 Hiking trail crosses bicycle trail.
- 2.3 Cross South Bandy Creek.
- 2.5 Veer right.
- 3.1 Intersection with TN-297. Go right on TN-297. (The park service asks that you ride single file near the white line.)
- 4.5 Bicycles turn right off TN-297. Look for four-by-four marker. (If you reach the West Entrance Trailhead, you have gone too far.)
- 4.6 Right turn onto old road that is shared with hikers. (Will see red arrowhead for hikers.)
- 4.9 Left turn off shared trail. Look for four-by-four marker. The next 1.5 miles is mainly single track.
- 5.8 Begin winding single track followed by a downhill.
- 6.4 Left turn at the bottom of hill. (May turn right for another lap.)
- 6.5 Cross North Bandy Creek.
- 6.8 Right turn onto gravel road for return to visitor center.
- 8.0 End at visitor center.

32

Cumberland Plateau Classic

Norris Dam State Park
Lake City—Careyville—Oneida
Big South Fork National River and Recreation Area

Of all the southern trans-state bicycle touring events, the Bicycle Ride Across Tennessee (BRAT) covers the most challenging terrain as it travels through the Appalachian Mountains in northeastern Tennessee. The ride from Norris Dam State Park to the Big South Fork National River and Recreation Area crosses through the rolling-to-mountainous terrain of the Cumberland Plateau, through elevations ranging from 1,400 to 1,700 feet. Although the route is intended as one day in a week-long excursion across the state, the Cumberland Plateau Classic can lay the foundation for an adventure-packed three- or four-day weekend featuring the rich and varied Big South Fork National River and Recreation Area.

The ride begins at the excellent Norris Dam State Park, which includes an elaborate Olympic-size swimming pool. Family members who do not bicycle could spend the better part of a summer day enjoying this facility before meeting up with the cyclists of the group at Bandy Creek Campground in the Big South Fork National River and Recreation Area.

Once everyone has regrouped at Bandy Creek Campground, a wide variety of activities, including more bike-riding possibilities, awaits the entire family. Horseback riding, hiking, and swimming are all within walking distance of the campground. Bandy Creek also features mountain-bike trails, which we have outlined in the preceding chapter, Big South Fork Ramble.

Those attempting the 64-mile BRAT route should be fine without support as the route passes through the towns of Lake City, Careyville, and Oneida before the final climb into Bandy Creek Campground. Although you'll find numerous country stores along the way, the route can seem extremely isolated at times as it wanders through Tennessee hill country of cornfields, pastures, and kudzu. Much of the route passes by mountains heavily forested in pines and hardwoods.

Touring bikes or mountain bikes may be best suited for the Cumberland Plateau Challenge. Early in the ride you will abandon pavement for gravel roads that wander for a good 6 miles alongside Cove Creek. A triple chain ring may be beneficial for the 13 percent grade that descends and climbs into the river gorge approaching Bandy Creek Campground. This 2.5-mile stretch, past rock crevice and the Cumberland River, provides the ultimate scenic reward of the ride. Although mountain bikes make for slower travel on paved sections, you will be glad you have them for exploration of the Bandy Creek compound.

If you enjoy bicycle touring from campground to campground, you might extend your tour beyond Bandy Creek Campground and on west just 15 miles farther to Pickett State Rustic Park off TN-154. The park has camping and cabin facilities with hiking, swimming, and cave exploration.

If you have not yet visited the Big South Fork National River and Recreation Area, we urge you to do so. Cycling the BRAT bicycle route will give you an appreciation for this rugged pocket of Tennessee. A full week would not be wasted exploring the area. Whitewater-rafting enthusiasts might well plan a trip for the fall to take advantage of peak water levels on the Cumberland River. Several outfitters lead rafting trips down the Big South Fork.

Load your mountain bike, and your canoe or kayak, and do the Big South Fork to the max.

The Basics

Start: The Cumberland Plateau Classic begins at the swimming pool parking lot of Norris Dam State Park. To get to the park, take I–75 North from Knoxville. Follow signs to the park.
Length: 64.2 miles.
Terrain: Rolling hills to mountainous. There is one 13 percent grade climb into Bandy Creek Campground.
Food: You will find country stores at 9.4, 25.1, 29.4, 31.0, 42.0, and 55.3 miles. You'll find restaurants in Lake City at 3.8 miles, Careyville at 9.4 miles, and Oneida at 50 miles.
For more information: Charlie Tate, Parks and Recreation, 701 Broadway, Nashville, TN 37219 (enclose a SASE).

Miles & Directions

- 0.0 Norris Dam State Park swimming pool parking lot.
- 0.1 Right turn.
- 0.6 Right onto Hwy. 441.
- 3.8 Entering Lake City. Right onto Hwy. 116 North.
- 9.4 Careyville city limits.
- 10.1 Left onto Hwy. 25W South; cross I–75, then go straight. **Caution: congested area.**
- 10.6 Road narrows.
- 11.9 Pavement changes. Rough road begins, but you'll have very little traffic.
- 12.7 Bridge crossing. Rough gravel surface begins.
- 13.3 Narrow bridge.
- 15.0 Railroad crossing.
- 15.3 Bridge crossing.
- 18.3 Bridge crossing in less than 0.1 mile.
- 18.4 **Caution: rough railroad crossing.**
- 19.0 Left onto Hwy. 63 (Howard Baker Hwy.). It has a wide, paved shoulder.
- 20.0 There'll be a fresh water spring on the right side of highway in less than 0.1 mile.

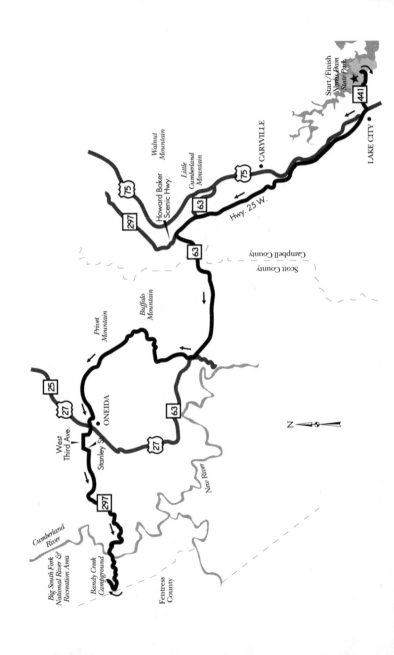

- 30.4 Right onto Hwy. 297 West.
- 33.1 Right turn. (Note there is a Handy Randy's on your left prior to making this turn.)
- 36.2 **Caution: Right side of the road is caved in.** Rough road begins.
- 37.1 Rough road ends.
- 49.3 Right turn onto Hwy. 297. Entering Oneida.
- 50.0 Right onto Bilbrey Rd.
- 50.1 Go straight across Hwy. 27.
- 50.4 Left onto West Third Ave.
- 50.5 Left onto Stanley St.
- 51.0 Begin Hwy. 297 West.
- 55.3 Terry & Terry Market. Go to your left.
- 59.3 Entrance to Big South Fork.
- 60.1 **Caution: Begin a 13-percent downgrade with switchbacks for 1.5 miles.**
- 61.6 **Caution: Begin a 13-percent upgrade with switchbacks for 1 mile.**
- 62.6 Right turn into Bandy Creek Campground.
- 64.2 Entering the Bandy Creek Visitor Center area.

33

Great Smoky Mountains Challenge

Cherokee—Oconaluftee Visitor Center—Smokemont
Clingmans Dome—Newfound Gap
Sugarlands Visitor Center—Gatlinburg

Newfound Gap Road (US-441) cuts an awesome path through the heart of Great Smoky Mountains National Park. It is a road of switchbacks past craggy gray overhangs and deep evergreen of fraser fir and red spruce. Mists can hover like spirits, and clear blue sky can bring the mountain peaks into sharp focus. Newfound Gap Road parallels the rolling, rocky waters of the Little Pigeon River on the Tennessee side and the Oconaluftee River on the North Carolina side. Throughout the fall season, hardwood forests of maple, yellow poplar, chestnut, and white oak lure tourists by the thousands. Newfound Gap Road leads the way to Clingmans Dome (elevation 6,642 feet) and Newfound Gap (elevation 5,048 feet). This is heady stuff for any bicyclist.

The Great Smoky Mountains Challenge identifies several options for crossing Great Smoky Mountains National Park. National Park Service maps very clearly outline roads within the park. Existing roads suggest a variety of day trips emanating from the handful of campgrounds and visitor centers in the park. You might cycle from campground to campground for an extended touring weekend, or you might park at Oconaluftee or Sugarlands Visitor Center

---

for an extended hill climb up to Clingmans Dome. If you decide to traverse the park on Newfound Gap Road, remember that the geology of the Smokies demands constant climbing to Newfound Gap followed by magnificent descents down either side.

The down side to all this cycling glory is, in a word, traffic. Weekends, holidays, and the entire fall season are times to *avoid, avoid, avoid* bicycling in Great Smoky Mountains National Park. Insignificant weekends are tolerable. Weekdays are the best choice for cycling in the park. With Newfound Gap Road as the main thoroughfare through the park, congestion problems are very real. Carbon monoxide, careless drivers, and excess people downgrade a potentially exalted cycling experience.

While the Great Smoky Mountains Challenge explores routes running through the park, make note of the Cades Cove Ramble, which offers an additional side trip in Great Smoky Mountains National Park.

The following are suggestions for tours across the park.

Clingmans Dome Hill Climb: Park at the overlook at Newfound Gap, and cycle up the side road 7 miles to Clingmans Dome for an intense hill climb and a runaway descent back down.

Assault on Clingmans Dome: Park at Sugarlands Visitor Center on the Tennessee side, or at Oconaluftee Visitor Center on the North Carolina side, and cycle the long ascent along Newfound Gap Road taking the side road up to Clingmans Dome. Coast back down to your starting point. Beware of tunnels and wild switchbacks on the Tennessee side.

Cherokee to Gatlinburg Tour: Cycle Newfound Gap Road from either Cherokee or Gatlinburg, do the town, spend the night, and cycle back through Great Smoky Mountains National Park. This is a primo 35-mile tour. Approaching the park from both directions will create a fascinating mirror image.

Lost in the Smokies Camping Getaway: Load up your touring, or mountain, bike with panniers and camping gear, and wander from campground to campground. Take a week or two. Smokemont, Elkmont, and Cades Cove campgrounds are accessible via Newfound Gap Road. Five other campgrounds are reached by other roads outlined on the park service map.

Balsam Mountain by Mountain Bike: From Oconaluftee Visitor Center, follow the Blue Ridge Parkway north to Balsam Mountain Road (this is *all* uphill). Follow Balsam Mountain Road to Balsam Mountain campground and Heintooga Overlook. Follow Round Bottom Road (unpaved gravel) to Big Cove Road (becomes paved) back along Newfound Gap Road (US-441) to Oconaluftee Visitor Center.

The Basics

Start: Great Smoky Mountains National Park. See the suggestions above for possible starting points.
Length: 7 to 35 miles.
Terrain: Mountainous.
Food: Carry plenty of water and food. There are very few outlets for food in the park.
For more information: Superintendent, Great Smoky Mountains National Park, Gatlinburg, TN 37738; (615) 436–1200.

34

Cades Cove Ramble

Great Smoky Mountains National Park

The Cades Cove Ramble is an 11-mile loop nestled in the middle of Great Smoky Mountains National Park. This is an ideal jaunt for cyclists of all levels. There's only one hitch: If your visit to the Smokies coincides with a Sunday, holiday weekend, or with the peak fall foliage season, forget about trying this ride.

The Cades Cove Loop Road is touted for bicyclists and motorists as a scenic tour of an Appalachian mountain community dating back to the early 1800s. A single-lane, one-way road, the loop travels through the lush green valley that supported a population of 685 in 1850. While you might cycle once around the loop just to get a workout, you'll want to follow the loop around a second time to explore the homesteads, churches, and Cable Mill. The National Park Service closes the road to motorized traffic on Saturday mornings from 6:00 to 10:00 A.M., making this precious, four-hour slot the ideal time to cycle the Cades Cove Ramble. Park service maps depict this and other roads within the park.

The folks at the bicycle rental service located at Cades Cove campground recommend cycling the loop on weekday mornings if you can't visit the park on a Saturday morning. *Biking in Cades Cove,* a brochure obtained in the shop, warns of steep hills, sharp curves, and the potential for accidents on the loop. You can even purchase a T-shirt with the fitting caption "I Survived Cades Cove"—only not for the technical difficulty of the ride. On a Sunday afternoon, the entire 11 miles may well have bumper-to-bumper traffic crawling at a pace most cyclists could match.

Bicyclists can truly gain the advantage by rising early to cycle this loop. Not only are the odds much greater that you will observe white-tailed deer, chipmunks, or even a black bear, but this may be the only time motorists will not ruin what is a fine, scenic cycling byway.

The Basics

Start: Cades Cove is 24 miles off US-441, which runs through Great Smoky Mountains National Park. You will turn at the Sugarlands Visitor Center and drive along the Little River. Just follow the signs to Cades Cove.
Length: 11 miles.
Terrain: Rolling with a few quick, steep hills.
Special conditions: Beware of a few rough spots in the road surface.
Food: There is a grocery store in the Cades Cove campground complex.
For more information: Superintendent, Great Smoky Mountains National Park, Gatlinburg, TN 37738; (615) 436–1200.

Miles & Directions

This is a simple 11-mile loop that begins just beyond the entrance to the Cades Cove Campground. You might want to pick up the *Biking in Cades Cove* brochure at the bicycle rental shop. The Great Smoky Mountains Natural History Association publishes *Cades Cove Auto Tour,* which can be purchased at the entrance to the loop for 25 cents.

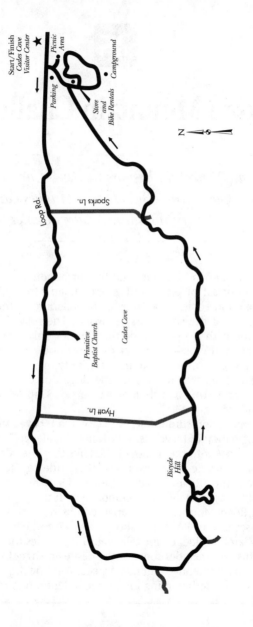

Start/Finish
Cades Cove
Visitor Center

Picnic
Area

Parking

Store
and
Bike Rentals

Campground

N

Loop Rd.

Sparks Ln.

Cades Cove

Primitive
Baptist Church

Hyatt Ln.

Bicycle
Hill

35

Roan Mountain Challenge

Roan Mountain Visitors Center—Carver's Gap
Glen Ayre—Buladean—Hughes Gap
Roan Mountain Visitors Center

In mid-June, Roan Mountain and the surrounding balds are a spectacular contrast of pinks and greens. Roan Mountain has more than six hundred acres of Catawba rhododendron—the largest natural garden of the species in the world. The rugged landscape of Roan Mountain is a popular destination not only for bicyclists, but for hikers and cross-country skiers, who flock to the network of trails at the summit of Roan. This network includes the Appalachian Trail, which traverses the ridge line of Roan Mountain and intersects this bicycle loop at Carvers Gap (elevation 5,512 feet) on Highway 143.

Any mountain summit accessible by road, paved or gravel, fires the imagination of bicyclists. Words like "challenge," "assault," and "attack" creep into the names of rides like this one. Members of the Kingsport Bicycle Association call their ride to the top of Roan Mountain the "Roan Groan." Club president Richard Heppert, in an accurate assessment of the climb, says, "It never lets up."

The Roan Mountain Challenge climbs to Carvers Gap on the Tennessee side of Roan and shoots down into Roan Valley on the North Carolina side. Ultimately, your loop circles the entire mountain. This ride includes some of the best elements of mountain cycling with an extended climb and steep, winding descents.

Although the blooming of the rhododendron is the most celebrated event at Roan Mountain, the Cherokee and Pisgah national forests provide a rich variety of foliage rewarding in each season. There are dramatic changes in the forests you pass through. As you begin your ride at the Roan Mountain Visitors Center, you are surrounded by the maple, sycamore, and oak of the cove hardwood forests characteristic of elevations in the 3,000-to-4,000-foot range. As you make your slow ascent up the mountain, there is time for deep gazes into lush woods with greens of every shade. Water tumbles down moss-covered creek beds in a descent to join the Doe River. Bluets, goldenrod, dandelions, and oxeye daisies line the roadside. By the time you round the last curve at Carvers Gap, the mountainside has graduated to stands of spruce and fraser fir. Looking east, the dark green leaves of rhododendron blanket the balds as your eye follows the Appalachian Trail into the horizon.

While the ascent to Roan Mountain is best approached as a meditation on the art of climbing, the descent and ramble through the Roan Valley make a fast-paced thrill. The descents are so steep and technical that you may find yourself focusing intensely in an effort to savor the experience. The thrill passes so quickly, you may find yourself regretting the speed while you are enjoying it.

The back stretch of the loop travels through the community of Buladean (that's Bula-dean), veering off to the right to climb Hughes Gap and descend once more toward the community of Roan Mountain. The back stretch contains a rough 1.5-mile gravel section. Factoring this with the steep descent from Carvers Gap, we recommend riding a mountain bike or a touring bike with touring tires. A mountain bike will give you better control on the descents—enough to relax and enjoy the ride. Racing bikes are not recommended for this tour unless you're up for a little cyclocross—you'll have to carry your bike up the gravel section to Hughes Gap.

Roan Mountain State Park is a delight. This ride could be incorporated into an outstanding weekend of camping, hiking, and bicycling. The state park campground is 2.5 miles into the loop, so you could cycle right out of your campsite. Campsites are at a premium on the weekends. Activities ranging from bluegrass music and clogging to trout-fishing tournaments are planned for every weekend throughout the summer and fall.

The Basics

Start: From Elk Park, Tenn. take US-19E heading north for 1.5 miles to the Tennessee state line. Continue 4.3 miles to the community of Roan Mountain. Turn left onto Hwy. 143 heading south. (You'll see signs for Roan Mountain State Park.) Park your vehicle at the visitors center on the left.

Length: 38.0 miles.

Terrain: Mountainous to rolling, with steep descents.

Food: There are country stores and/or restaurants in Glen Ayre at 17.0 miles, Buladean at 27.4, and Cove Creek at 33.7.

Special conditions: Mountain bikes may be the best bike for this tour. Use extreme caution on the descents and the gravel stretch at Hughes Gap.

Miles & Directions

- **0.0** Parking lot of the Roan Mountain State Park Visitors Center. Head south toward Roan Mountain on Hwy. 143.
- **2.5** Roan Mountain campground on the right.
- **6.6** Twin Springs Overlook and Picnic Area. The grade eases off a bit from here.
- **10.8** Carvers Gap (elev. 5,512 feet). The Appalachian Trail intersects Hwy. 143 and heads east over the bald. Hwy. 143 becomes Hwy. 261. Get ready for the big descent.
- **17.0** Entering Glen Ayre community.
- **17.6** Five Oaks Campground.
- **19.6** Turn right onto Fork Mountain Rd. just before the bridge.
- **23.7** Turn right onto Hwy. 226.
- **27.4** Entering Buladean community.
- **27.6** Turn right at the Exxon gas station. (You should have passed a school on your right before this intersection.) This road is known as Hughes Gap Rd., but it is not marked.
- **30.8** Bear right onto a gravel road. You will climb for 1.5 miles to Hughes Gap.
- **31.9** The road becomes paved. (Beyond Hughes Gap the road

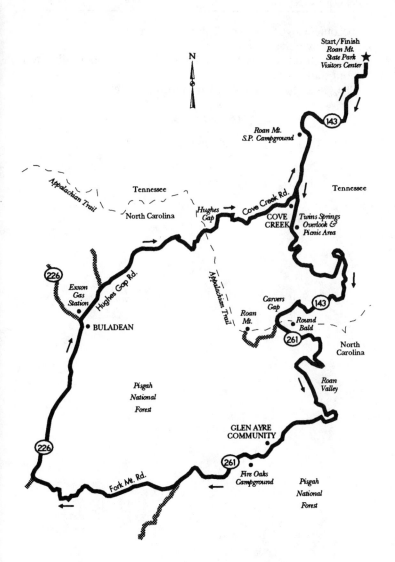

becomes Cove Creek Rd.) This is very steep.

- 33.7 Cove Creek community.
- 34.8 Left onto Hwy. 143 North. You are less than 4 miles from your starting point.
- 38.0 Roan Mountain State Park Visitors Center.

36

Meriwether Lewis Ramble

Meriwether Lewis Visitors Center
Natchez Trace Parkway

In 1809 American explorer Meriwether Lewis fell ill at Grinder's Inn, just yards from where this ride begins, ultimately dying under "mysterious" circumstances. Mysterious could well describe the atmosphere all along the Natchez Trace Parkway, a 400-mile road that follows the route of an original footpath, "The Old Trace," first traveled by Chickasaw and Choctaw Indians.

A mere 22-mile bike ride along the Natchez Trace will immerse you in a multilayered history ranging from Indian prehistory to the travels of frontiersmen and Mississippi River boatmen in the early 1800s to an iron-mining industry that thrived up to World War I.

The route follows an out-and-back course over gently rolling hills with a 2.5-mile detour onto a section of the original Trace. Ten miles traveled easily by bicycle in an hour or so might have been half a day's journey for the men and women who traveled the Old Trace. It was used by Post-Riders, who could carry the mail from Nashville, Tennessee, to Natchez, Mississippi, in ten days. Mississippi River boatmen called "Kaintucks" took their flatboats down river, then walked the Old Trace back up to Nashville. The Trace was also utilized as a main thoroughfare by the soldiers of three major American conflicts—the French and Indian War, the War of 1812, and the Civil War. Other notable travelers included circuit-riding preachers and thieves.

Exhibits erected along the parkway effectively illustrate the potential hazards along the way. The Metal Ford Exhibit at mile 3.5 details the processes of an ironworks. This is also the site of McLish's Stand, an inn that welcomed travelers along the Trace. The stream and shade trees here make an excellent picnic spot.

Cycling the Natchez Trace Parkway allows bicyclists special insight into the trials of early travel in the region. A soupy humidity permeates the atmosphere impacting every movement. In the physical world, some things never change: In 1807 Harman Blennerhassett wrote, "I can adjust a simple handkerchief about my head and face in a way to parry the mosquitoes, or their more formidable companions the horseflies." Yes, insects are still a menace. Did you know insect repellent will eat holes right through Lycra cycling shorts?

A few years later, in 1811, Alexander Lewis described the area this way: "I passed through the most horrid swamps I had ever seen. These are covered with a prodigious growth of canes, and high woods, which . . . shut out almost the whole light of day for miles." The 2.5-mile stretch along the Old Trace remains fully canopied by trees, although the swamps Mr. Lewis speaks of actually are found a bit south of this route.

In spite of these difficulties, the Natchez Trace Parkway provides excellent cycling opportunities all along its length. Countless rides can be undertaken suitable to all levels and abilities. Simply pick an interesting point, and cycle out from there. You will find several other rides incorporating the Natchez Trace Parkway in the Mississippi section.

The Basics

Start: Begin at the Meriwether Lewis Exhibit Parking Area just off the Natchez Trace Parkway at milepost 385.9. The northern terminus of the Natchez Trace Parkway is located about 40 miles south of Nashville, Tenn.
Length: 22.0 miles.
Terrain: Flat to gently rolling.
Food: Water and rest rooms are the only facilities available along

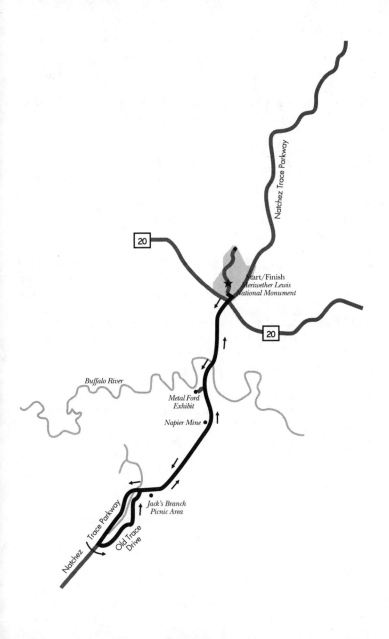

the route; there are soda machines at Meriwether Lewis. The town of Hohenwald, just 7 miles west on TN-20, has several restaurants and stores.

For more information: Superintendent, Natchez Trace Parkway, Rural Rte. 1, NT-143, Tupelo, MS 38801; (601) 842–1572.

Miles & Directions

- 0.0 Meriwether Lewis Exhibit Parking Area.
- 0.1 Left following signs for the Natchez Trace Parkway.
- 0.4 Head south on the parkway toward Tupelo.
- 3.5 Metal Ford Exhibit.
- 4.5 Napier Mine.
- 8.3 Jack's Branch Picnic Area (water and rest rooms here).
- 10.3 Entrance to the Old Trace Drive. Turn left, and follow the original Natchez Trace north (several scenic overlooks of the valley along the way).
- 12.8 A cloverleaf takes you back up to the parkway. Just before you exit the scenic drive, you will ford Jack's Branch, a 2-foot-wide stream. Take off your socks and shoes, and cool your feet.
- 13.7 Jack's Branch Picnic Area.
- 16.8 Napier Mine.
- 17.8 Metal Ford.
- 20.9 Exit left off the Natchez Trace Parkway into Meriwether Lewis.
- 21.9 Turn right back to exhibits parking area.
- 22.0 Back at the parking lot.

Virginia

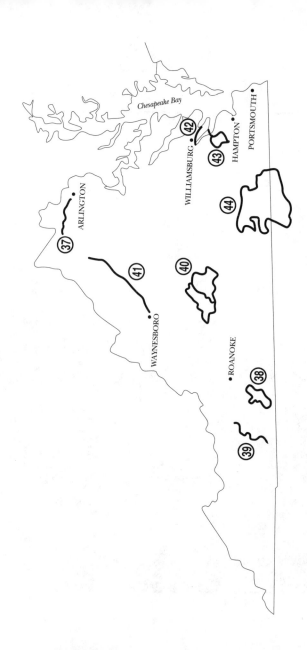

Chesapeake Bay

PORTSMOUTH

HAMPTON

42

WILLIAMSBURG

43

44

ARLINGTON

37

41

40

WAYNESBORO

ROANOKE

38

39

Virginia

Washington & Old Dominion Cruise

Alexandria—Falls Church—Reston—Herndon
Ashburn—Leesburg—Purcellville—Bluemont

In the midst of the congestion of Washington, D.C., and Fairfax County, a paved bicycle trail spans 45 miles west from Alexandria, Virginia, into the northern Virginia countryside. A Sunday afternoon on the Washington & Old Dominion Trail demonstrates the "greenway" concept in action. Bicyclists, walkers, runners, horseback riders, roller-blade skaters, and other human-powered travelers can all be found enjoying this linear park.

The W&OD is a Rails-To-Trails Conservancy project constructed in conjunction with the Northern Virginia Regional Park Authority. The park authority maintains the 45-mile W&OD Trail and publishes an excellent strip map outlining the trail for $4.50. Don't let visions of chaos on a multi-use byway turn you off. While use is heavy on weekends, the western end of the trail, from Leesburg to Purcellville, is less congested.

The Potomac Pedalers include the W&OD in their repertoire of regular rides. On the Saturday morning we set out, a group of a dozen or so was headed out for lunch in Purcellville. The horse farms of Loudoun County grace either side of the trail with their rolling green pastures.

Railroad lore is ever present on the W&OD. The Herndon Museum and Depot provides an impressive historical presentation of the Washington & Old Dominion Railroad and the development of Fairfax County. The birth of the town of Herndon can be traced back to the arrival of the railroad around 1857. Displays feature railroad paraphernalia including tools, uniforms, and local dress, photographs, a telegraph machine, and a beacon alighting one of the original trains.

The cycling possibilities along the W&OD are numerous. If you're visiting the D.C. area, day trips require a minimum of effort and planning. The trail guide outlines parking facilities at each access point along the route. If you've chosen Fairfax County as your base camp, you should have no problem finding your way to the trail. Reston, Herndon, and Leesburg are all highly recommended as starting points.

If you're interested in overnight touring, cycle west from any of these points to Purcellville, and possibly on to Bears Den American Youth Hostel just 9 miles beyond the end of the trail. You'll find motels in Purcellville and a bed and breakfast in nearby Round Hill.

The Basics

Start: You have a choice of starting points along the W&OD. Parking areas are outlined in the trail guide. Alexandria, Falls Church, Vienna, Reston, Herndon, Ashburn, Leesburg, and Purcellville all make great starting points.
Length: The trail is 44.0 miles in length. An overnight tour from Herndon to Bears Den Hostel in Bluemont is 36.0 miles.
Terrain: Flat with a few short hills. For those traveling to Bears Den Hostel, there's a bit more climbing in store. The quarter-mile just before the entrance to the hostel is quite a challenge.
Food: There are many country stores and restaurants in the towns along the way. The restaurants and pubs in Leesburg at mile 33, along King St., date back to the mid-1800s and are especially inviting. Located at the western end of the trail, Purcellville, at mile 44, is an obvious lunch spot. There are several restaurants adjacent to the trail's end. You might venture west on Rte. 7 to the elegant Purcellville Inn.

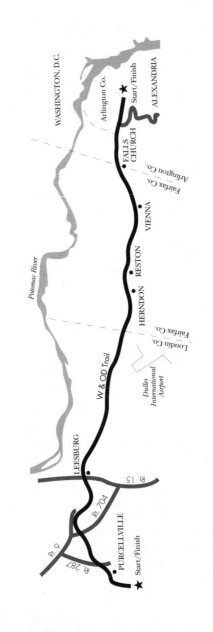

Special conditions: As with all bicycle trails, observe trail etiquette. Use caution when approaching others on the trail, and give pedestrians special consideration. Sound a warning when passing, and take care at intersections.

For more information: Northern Virginia Regional Park Authority, 5400 Ox Rd., Fairfax Station, VA 22039; (703) 689–1437. Bears Den Hostel, Rte. 1, Box 288, Bluemont, VA 22012; (703) 554–8708.

Miles & Directions

We're leaving the orienteering up to you. If you have chosen to cycle beyond Purcellville to Round Hill or Bears Den Hostel in Bluemont, take note of the directions that follow.

From the trail's end in Purcellville—

- 0.0 Turn left on 22nd St.
- 0.2 Turn right onto Rte. 7 West. On the outskirts of Purcellville, follow Business Rte. 7 through the town of Round Hill.
- 7.0 CR-760 intersects Rte. 7. Continue straight on Rte. 7 West to Bears Den. (Turn left for a half-mile side trip to the Snickersville General Store established in 1846.)
- 8.8 Turn left onto Rte. 601 (Blueridge Mt. Rd.). Get ready to shift into your granny gears for a steep, steep climb.
- 9.5 The driveway to Bears Den American Youth Hostel is on the right.

38

Floyd County Challenge

Floyd—Chateau Morrisette Winery
Rocky Knob—Tuggle Gap—Floyd

Extensive bicycling throughout the Blue Ridge uncovers an astounding maze of country back roads in Virginia. A glance at a Floyd County map reveals, on a smaller scale, a similar network of gravel and paved roads intersecting the countryside. Consequently it was not difficult to choose county routes for both mountain bikes and touring bikes.

Both routes begin at the stoplight in the town of Floyd, a friendly town within hollerin' distance of the Blue Ridge Parkway, and have their midway point at Chateau Morrisette Winery. The routes diverge on the back stretch. Mountain bikers can kick up the dust on the winding, gravel back roads, while those choosing touring bikes will enjoy a downhill run on the Blue Ridge Parkway.

The first 13 miles feature an uphill climb to the crest of the Blue Ridge and Chateau Morrisette Winery. With climbs inevitable in the Blue Ridge, it helps to keep in mind that this tour gets the dirty work over with in the first half of the ride. Touring bikes and mountain bikes are recommended for the Floyd County Challenge due to a 2-mile gravel stretch common to both routes.

Chateau Morrisette is one of more than forty farm wineries in Virginia. Most famous for their "Sweet Mountain Laurel," their tour and wine tasting acquaints you with all of the Morrisette wines, from Chardonnay to White Riesling to Merlot. In the summer the grounds of the winery invite you to lounge in Adirondack chairs amid country gardens full of poppies, gladiolus, and lilies.

From Chateau Morrisette the touring-bike route joins the Blue Ridge Parkway in the Rocky Knob area. The terrain of Rocky Knob is often compared to the Scottish Highlands. The parkway winds between broad, grassy knobs strewn with countless boulders and grazing cattle. If you gaze high up to the isolated fir, you can almost make out a lone bagpiper in his Black Watch kilt bellowing into the wind. From Rocky Knob campground you will enjoy a long downhill run into the valley. Unlike the mountain-bike travelers, those opting for the touring-bike route may be able to get a bit carried away with the wine tasting. You do a lot more coasting on the way back to Floyd than those exploring the gravel path.

A series of steep, gravel roads meander their way back to Floyd for the mountain bikers. In addition to the challenge of negotiating steep switchbacks with mad dog curves, your route takes one step back from the picture-postcard perfection of the Blue Ridge Parkway onto roads that pass the family farms and homesteads of the local residents. The final 4 miles on Route 615 are paved back to Floyd.

Both routes pass the crossroads of Tuggle Gap with its restaurant and motel. Here either route may be shortened by taking Highway 8 North back to Floyd.

The final stretch of the touring-bike route turns off the parkway onto Route 860. This turn is hard to miss with The Wormy Chestnut Country Crafts placed strategically at this junction. If you like mountain crafts, The Wormy Chestnut Country Crafts is crammed with baskets, pottery, quilts, and other hand-crafted items. In July and August the final swing back to Floyd on Route 860 is framed in thousands of feathery blue chicory blooms.

Once back in Floyd, take some time to coast, or walk, through town. Stop in at the Harvest Moon Foodstore and Cockram's General Store. Stocking a variety of goods from "bib overalls to potted possum," Cockram's also has a regular "Friday Nite Jamboree," where musicians are invited to bring their mandolins, fiddles, banjos, and guitars for a lively session of mountain pickin'.

If you want to get into the full spirit of the Floyd County Challenge, make a weekend of it. Spend Friday night at The Pine Tavern

Lodge in Floyd, so you can stomp your feet at Cockram's on Friday night, then head out early Saturday morning for an all-day, grand pedal of the countryside.

The Basics

Start: Begin at the single stoplight in downtown Floyd, Va. To get to Floyd from the Blue Ridge Parkway, take Hwy. 8 North to Floyd; from Roanoke take the Blue Ridge Parkway or Hwy. 21 South. From I–81 take Hwy. 21 North.

Length: Touring-bike route, 31.3 miles; mountain-bike route, 28.5.

Terrain: Rolling to mountainous; one extended climb to Chateau Morrisette Winery.

Food: At 12.9 miles, Chateau Morrisette Winery serves lunch and dinner, but with very limited hours: lunch 11:00 A.M.–2:00 P.M.; dinner 6:00–9:00 P.M. (reservations required). There are stores and restaurants in Floyd (0.0) and Tuggle Gap (19.7). The Wormy Chestnut Country Crafts at mile 25.7 sells soft drinks.

Miles & Directions

Touring- and mountain-bike routes are the same to Chateau Morrisette Winery.

- 0.0 Downtown Floyd, Va. Begin at the intersection of Hwy. 221 and Hwy. 8 (at the single traffic light in town). Head south on Hwy. 221.
- 0.7 Turn left onto Rte. 720.
- 1.6 Rte. 720 becomes a hard-packed, gravel road. The gravel road continues for 2 miles.
- 3.6 Turn left and take the jag, 0.2 mile, to Rte. 807.
- 3.8 Turn right onto Rte. 807.
- 5.5 Left onto Rte. 726. The toughest climb of the tour commences here. Rte. 727 climbs up to the Blue Ridge.
- 12.5 Turn right onto Rte. 777 (Winery Rd.).
- 12.9 Chateau Morrisette Winery.

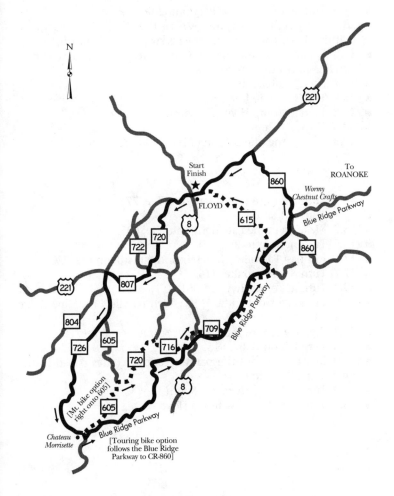

N

221

To
ROANOKE

Start
Finish

★

FLOYD

860

Wormy
Chestnut Crafts

Blue Ridge Parkway

8

722

720

615

860

221

807

804

726

605

720

709

716

Blue Ridge Parkway

8

[Mt. bike option
right onto 605]

605

Chateau
Morrisette

Blue Ridge Parkway

[Touring bike option
follows the Blue Ridge
Parkway to CR-860]

For the touring-bike option—

- 12.9 Turn left from the winery onto Rte. 777.
- 13.1 Turn right onto Rte. 726 to the Blue Ridge Parkway (within view). Turn left onto the parkway heading north.
- 15.9 Rocky Knob Information Center on left (water, rest rooms, and literature available here).
- 19.7 Hwy. 8 intersects here.
- 25.7 Turn left onto Hwy. 860.
- 28.6 Turn left onto Hwy. 221 South.
- 30.6 Floyd city limits.
- 31.3 Back at the intersection of Hwy. 221 and Hwy. 8.

For the mountain-bike option—

- 12.9 Turn left from the winery onto Rte. 777.
- 13.1 Turn left onto Rte. 726.
- 13.2 Make an immediate right onto Rte. 605.
- 15.5 Turn right onto Rte. 720.
- 17.5 Just past Fairview Church bear right (still on Rte. 720).
- 17.7 Turn right onto Rte. 716.
- 19.4 Turn left onto Hwy. 8 North.
- 19.8 Turn right onto Rte. 709, which parallels the Blue Ridge Parkway.
- 21.3 Rte. 709 crosses the parkway; bear left onto Rte. 709.
- 23.6 Turn left onto Rte. 615.
- 24.0 Rte. 615 crosses the parkway and becomes paved in the final stretch back to Floyd.
- 28.0 Turn left onto Hwy. 221 South.
- 28.5 You're back in downtown Floyd.

39

New River Trail Cruise

Galax—Fries—Byllesby Dam—Ivanhoe—Austinville
Shot Tower—Foster Falls—Loneash—Allisonia
Hiwassee—Draper—Pulaski

A bicycle tour along the New River Trail can take you back fifty or sixty years; it can also take you back more than 100 million years. It all depends upon your perspective and the elasticity of your imagination. The New River of West Virginia and Virginia is the second-oldest river in the world. Once part of the vast Teays River, the New dates back geologically more than 100 million years to a time when the Appalachian Mountains towered among the highest mountain ranges on Earth. For a time in prehistory, the Teays was more than 1,000 miles long, extending from North Carolina northwestward across Virginia, West Virginia, Ohio, Indiana, and Illinois. Get out on the trail, scan the water rushing past high rock cliffs, and ponder that for a moment.

Too far back for comprehension? Well, you don't have to pedal far to see clear, tangible evidence of a once-thriving railroad culture. The Norfolk & Western Railroad supported commerce through the Appalachians dating back to the twenties and thirties. There are two tunnels and three major bridges to remind you that a railroad once roared alongside the river, rattled across bridges, and whistled through these tunnels. There are abandoned mills and industrial sites, such as the Fries Textile Plant and the Austinville Limestone Company.

Virginia's state park system has created something rare and precious for mountain bikers, an isolated trail of supreme scenic beauty that welcomes fat-tire adventurers. The New River Trail State Park, "Virginia's only linear State Park," features the converted railroad bed of the Norfolk & Western Line. Designed for horseback riders, hikers, cross-country skiers, and mountain bikers, the New River Trail is part of a nationwide "greenway" movement. The conversion of abandoned railroad lines across the country is the brainchild of the nonprofit, Rails-To-Trails Conservancy headquartered in Washington, D.C.

When the New River Trail is finished, you will be able to travel 51.5 miles from Galax, Virginia, to Pulaski, Virginia, with a 5.5-mile spur diverging off the main trail to Fries. The 12-mile stretch just north of the park headquarters from Shot Tower State Historical Park to Allisonia is unfinished, effectively cutting off the trail at its midpoint. With this current stage of development, there are four recommended options for bicycle tours: Shot Tower State Historical Park to Galax, Shot Tower State Historical Park to Fries, Fries to Galax, or Pulaski to Allisonia. You can create any sort of ride you feel like along the trail, but these routes suggest destinations and possible overnight options.

Whatever your ambition, be prepared for a backwoods cycling experience. The New River Trail transports you away from the city, away from cars and trucks, off the asphalt, and into a world of hemlock, white pine, and rhododendron, rolling pastures and high ridges. Incredibly, you will pedal within yards of the New River for the majority of your journey. You will cross the New River numerous times on newly restored wooden bridges that were once railroad trestles. There are more than thirty bridges and trestles in all.

If you're looking to jump logs and careen around hairpin turns, this may not be the mountain bike ride you're expecting. The terrain is so tame, we hope you won't be disappointed. The secret of this ride lies in the serenity of the New River. We hope you get so caught up in the spinning round and round of your two feet, in the head rush of propelling yourself deep into the woods, in the crisp breeze and the babbling waters that you completely forget about the two wheels beneath you.

The Basics

Start: You will find trailheads with parking in the Virginia towns of Galax, Fries, Ivanhoe, and Pulaski. *Galax:* proceed north through town on Hwy. 89 (Main St.). Hwy. 89 North turns right onto Stuart Dr. Look for a New River Trail State Park signage just ahead on the left. *Fries:* From Galax go south on Hwy. 89. Bear right onto Rte. 94 (follow the signs to Fries). The trail begins on Main St. in the center of Fries (across from the Colonial Inn). *Ivanhoe:* Take Rte. 94 to Rte. 743; go west on 743 approximately 200 feet to park entrance. *Shot Tower Historical State Park:* From I–77 take exit 5; go east on Rte. 69 to Rte. 52; turn left onto Rte. 52 and follow signs to Shot Tower. *Pulaski:* From I–81 take Rte. 99 west for approximately 2 miles. Turn right on Saley Rd. Trailhead is .1 mile ahead.

Length: Ultimately 57.0 miles of trail await you. Suggested options include 26.2-, 20-, 17-, and 10.6-mile sections of the trail. Conquer the whole thing, or relax and go as far as your spirit takes you.

Terrain: Originally engineered as a railroad line, the trail is relatively flat with an occasional, slight uphill grade.

Food: Bring plenty of water and food. There are no facilities on the trail; you will have to detour off the trail to find stores in the small towns along the way.

For more information: New River Trail State Park, Rte. 1, Box 81X, Austinville, VA 24312; (703) 699–6778.

Miles & Directions

Shot Tower Historical State Park to Galax (26.2 miles one way): Plan for a full day's excursion or an overnight in Galax. The trail deposits you right in the center of town, where you will find several restaurants and motels.

Shot Tower Historical State Park to Fries (20 miles one way): From Shot Tower you take the Spur trail to Fries at Fries Junction (bear right). If you cross the Fries Junction bridge, you've gone too far. Fries is a tiny mill town with two small restaurants and a possible bed and breakfast inn. Call before attempting an overnight here.

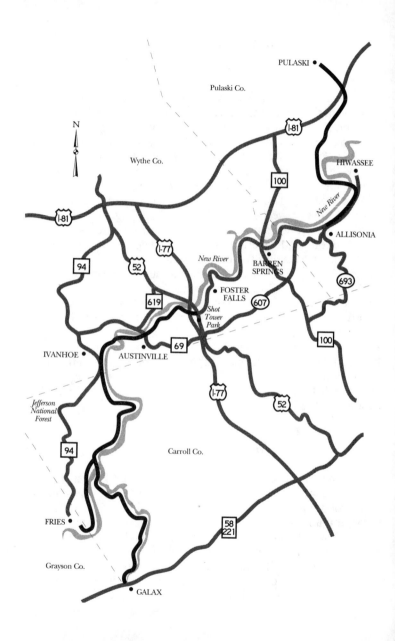

Fries to Galax (17 miles): Combining the Fries spur with the first leg of the trail from Galax makes a nice day trip out and back. Have lunch in either town.

Pulaski to Allisonia (10.6 miles): Ride out and back from Pulaski for a great day trip.

40

Storming of Thunder Ridge Classic

Lynchburg—Boonsboro—Big Island
Peaks of Otter—Otterville
Cifax—Lynchburg

Imagine a bike ride that begins on narrow, country roads canopied with birch, oaks, poplar, and hickory. You pedal along breathing in morning air scented with fresh-cut hay and honeysuckle. After wandering this maze of back roads for an hour or so, you find yourself cycling straight-on toward the Blue Ridge. When you pedal, finally, onto the Blue Ridge Parkway, you find your pulse beating to the rhythm—Thunder Ridge . . . Thunder Ridge. On and on you find yourself climbing. Then, just when you think you can bear no more, you crest the Blue Ridge at Apple Orchard Mountain (at 3,950 feet, the highest point on the parkway in Virginia) and hurl yourself and your bike into a long, winding descent to the picturesque Peaks of Otter Lodge accented by the sister peaks, Flat Top and Sharp Top. From the Peaks of Otter, you turn off the Blue Ridge Parkway and head down the mountain, back into that maze of country back roads.

Each September several hundred cyclists take part in the "Storming of Thunder Ridge." Pioneered by the Central Virginia Bicycle Club of Lynchburg, this epic ride has evolved into a fund-raiser conducted by the American Lung Association of Virginia. Not the highest elevation in the Blue Ridge, but formidable in its own right, Thunder Ridge culminates at 3,948 feet on the Blue Ridge Parkway. The Lung Association offers several routes for cyclists of varying abilities.

We outline the 50- and 75-mile options. The 50-mile route stops short of the Blue Ridge Parkway and meanders through the valley just to the east of the Blue Ridge. Both rides have their difficulties, due to rolling hills and mountainous terrain, although the 50-mile route relieves a little bit of the pressure. They follow the same roads up to the junction of Hwy. 501 and Hwy. 122 within 2 miles of the Blue Ridge Parkway. This gives you ample opportunity to bail out of the longer route.

This ride can be appreciated on so many levels. For sheer athleticism it ranks right up there with mountainous climbs and all measure of hill in between. If you're out to experience the local culture, you won't be disappointed. On the 50-mile loop, the country store in Sedalia invites you to pull a milk can up to the bar and sip your Snapple cranberry-apple juice while studying the wooden plank floor and flour-sack curtains dating back to the 1940s. Then, there's the Suck Mountain Baptist Church. Ride a few miles pondering the derivation of that one.

Anyone who is happy just gazing upon gorgeous mountain vistas will easily feel fulfilled pedaling along pondering beauty, botany, geology, and all that green, green, green.

This ride is so appealing you might want to spread it out over an entire weekend. There are two lodging opportunities that make for great weekend excursions. The obvious lodging choice is Peaks of Otter Lodge. A stay at this mountain retreat should be enough to dispel any doubts about your ability to make that final push up Apple Orchard Mountain. The lodge serves southern-style, country meals—things like rainbow trout, country ham, and fried chicken. After dinner you might walk around the lake looking for white-tailed deer in the meadow.

Just a bit farther on the loop, you'll find Otter's Den Bed and Breakfast along Hwy. 43 toward Bedford. Otter's Den is a renovated, eighteenth-century, chestnut log cabin with two guest rooms. If you're eager to try something just off the beaten path, this is a perfect getaway.

However you decide to storm Thunder Ridge, this ride is worth making special plans for.

The Basics

Start: The ride begins at Jefferson Forest High School on the edge of Lynchburg. From US-221 take Perrowville Rd. (CR-663) 0.4 miles to the high school. If you're traveling from Bedford on US-221 this is a left-hand turn; from Lynchburg, a right turn. There's plenty of parking.

Length: 52.8 or 74.7 miles.

Terrain: Rolling hills to mountainous with an extended climb on the Blue Ridge Parkway.

Food: Country stores in Boonsboro at 18.0 miles, Big Island at 28.8, Bryant's Grocery at 61.5. Hold out for lunch at Peaks of Otter Lodge (51.4). Those opting for the 50-mile route will welcome a break at the Sedalia Country Store at 34.9 along US-122.

For more information: American Lung Association of Virginia, Central Region, 725 Church St., 10th Floor, Lynchburg, VA 24504; (800) 243–TREK.

Miles & Directions

- 0.0 Jefferson Forest High School. Turn right onto CR-663.
- 4.0 Right onto CR-644.
- 7.3 Right onto CR-621.
- 10.0 Around mile 10 take care on the descent. Watch out for rough pavement and a few large potholes.
- 13.0 Left onto CR-660. Be careful at this intersection.
- 15.3 Straight on CR-659 (CR-660 veers left).
- 17.0 Right onto CR-644 (Coffee Rd.).
- 18.0 Left onto Hwy. 501. Traffic increases on this highway.
- 27.9 Entering Big Island.
- 28.5 *The 52.8-mile route turns left onto US-122, while the 75-mile route continues straight.*

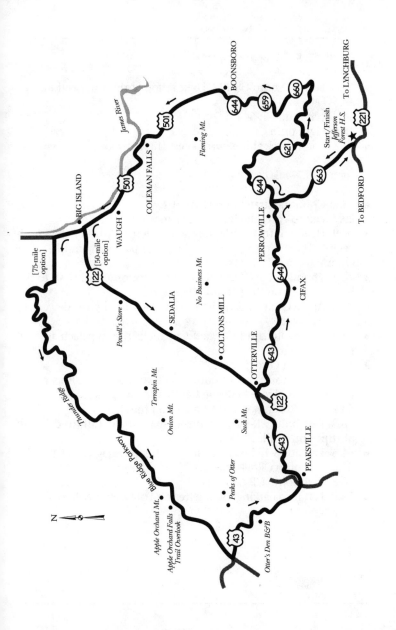

For the 52.8-mile option—

- 28.5 Turn left onto US-122. Use caution at this intersection.
- 39.6 Left onto CR-643.
- 44.9 Left onto CR-644.
- 48.9 Right onto CR-663.
- 52.8 You're back at Jefferson Forest High School.

For the 74.7-mile option—

- 28.5 Continue straight on Hwy. 501.
- 29.7 Left to enter the Blue Ridge Parkway.
- 29.9 Head south on the parkway (a left turn). Let the climb begin! (There are no facilities along the parkway until Peaks of Otter.)
- 40.5 Thunder Ridge Overlook. You've got one final push to the highest point on the parkway in Virginia.
- 42.5 Apple Orchard Mountain. Get ready for a great descent to Peaks of Otter.
- 44.4 Apple Orchard Falls Trail Overlook. The Appalachian Trail passes through here.
- 51.4 Peaks of Otter Lodge.
- 51.8 Left onto Hwy. 43 South. You'll turn at the visitors center and gift shop. From here you have a very fast descent.
- 53.9 Otter's Den Bed and Breakfast on the right.
- 56.8 Left onto CR-643. **Caution: sharp turn followed by an abrupt downhill.**
- 61.5 Left at US-122 North. Take a right at the jag onto CR-643.
- 66.8 Left onto CR-644.
- 70.8 Right onto CR-663.
- 74.7 Left into parking lot of Jefferson Forest High School.

41

Skyline Drive Classic

Front Royal—Skyland—Big Meadows
Loft Mountain—Waynesboro

Each September the Baltimore Bicycle Club sponsors an annual weekend tour of the Blue Ridge Mountains called the Skyline Drive Twin Century. At 105 miles in length, the Skyline Drive makes for a perfect century ride. There are no route changes, and the speed limit is a mere 35-miles per hour. You simply point your bike toward the blue haze and head for the highlands.

The Skyline Drive makes a gradual ascent from Front Royal to the ridge line of the Blue Ridge, which levels out to elevations in the 3,000-foot range. Impressions of the Blue Ridge vary greatly depending upon the season. Spring is a study in greens as hemlock, yellow birch, tulip poplar, red maple, and yellow maple burst forth in a growing frenzy. Every leaf is pert and fresh. Midsummer finds the foliage lush and mature. The trees along the Skyline Drive form many lovely canopies that make fall especially picturesque.

If 100-mile days sound daunting, Shenandoah National Park offers options for lodge-to-lodge touring. Big Meadows is among the finest rustic lodges in the Blue Ridge proper with a massive stone fireplace in the great room and a taproom featuring folksinging and bluegrass for after-dinner lounging. Dawn and dusk walks, through the meadow for which the lodge is named, assure deer sightings year-round and blueberry picking in the summer. At the 50-mile mark, Big Meadows divides the Skyline Drive perfectly for bicycle touring.

With Skyland Lodge, Big Meadows, and accommodations in Waynesboro, you could enjoy a leisurely week-long bicycle tour of the Skyline Drive with plenty of time for hiking and exploring. A survey of the views at overlooks along the way features numerous vistas of the Shenandoah Valley and peaks with a wide assortment of names: Marys Rock, Pinnacles, Stoney Man Mountain, Hawksbill Gap, and Bacon Hollow.

Although we have suggested the Skyline Drive as a classic ride, riders of all abilities can cycle it. Simply pick a starting point, and take off on as long a ride as you like. Remember that every descent you enjoy will have to be climbed on the way back. If you're new to mountain cycling, test your mettle on a few climbs before you venture too far.

The Basics

Start: You can park at the visitors center in Front Royal, but the National Park Service asks that you notify a park ranger if leaving your car overnight.

Length: 105 miles with many variations for shorter day trips.

Terrain: Hilly to mountainous.

Food: Food and water are available at the lodges and campgrounds along the way. You're never more than 20 miles from a restaurant or camp store.

Miles & Directions

It's difficult to be led astray along the Skyline Drive. Mileposts mark each mile running north to south. For a detailed map, contact: Superintendent, Shenandoah National Park, Luray, VA 22835; (703) 999–2266.

42

Colonial Parkway Cruise

Yorktown—Williamsburg—Jamestown Island

The year 1991 proved to be a banner year for bicycling in the Colonial Williamsburg area. The League of American Wheelmen chose the area for its annual GEAR rally of cyclists nationwide, while the American Lung Association of Virginia hosted hundreds of bicyclists in October for its annual Colonial Virginia Bike Trek. The Colonial Parkway was a primary bicycle route for both of these events.

Spanning 23 miles—from the York River port of Yorktown to Jamestown Island, which first attracted settlers sailing up the James River in 1607—the Colonial Parkway is a scenic byway connecting a tremendous amount of early American history. Granted, the cities themselves are the primary focus for travelers in the area, but bicycles are certainly a fitting way to explore these historic areas.

When you pedal into Williamsburg, even on the most high-tech racing machine, you've slowed your pace. For many of us the simple act of slowing down intensifies our perception, as we bring ourselves closer to the speeds characteristic of the time. Bicycle wheels bump down cobblestone streets with as much jolt as a horse-drawn carriage.

The National Park Service maintains the Colonial Parkway and enforces bicycle-friendly traffic laws. The speed limit is forty-five miles per hour, and commercial traffic is prohibited. While there is no shoulder, the two-lane highway actually has a third passing lane that adds considerable width to the road. In addition to these considerations, mileposts mark the mileage along the way. The park service requires bicyclists to ride single file, and this rule is enforced equally with the speed limit.

The National Park Service publishes an excellent map of the Colonial Parkway, outlining the route, loops into the historic cities, important sites, and geographical features throughout the area.

As the name Tidewater implies, the entire area is surrounded by water. Inland waterways form a network of creeks, rivers, and lakes. Two-thirds of the route travels alongside glistening water busy with aquatic activity. While bicycling offers its own special view, one can't help but think that boating or sailing is the true manner of exploration in the area.

In addition to the National Park Service map, the Virginia Department of Highways and Transportation publishes a map recommending detailed routes through Williamsburg, Yorktown, and beyond to York River State Park.

To plan a tour of the Colonial Parkway, simply decide what you want to see, and take off. You might treat yourself to an inn-to-inn weekend tour cycling from Yorktown to Williamsburg and Jamestown Island. You could set up headquarters in Williamsburg and radiate out from there. While Williamsburg is obviously the most popular of the three cities, the Yorktown waterfront rivals the charm of Williamsburg—you may even prefer it if you're hoping to avoid excessive crowds. For even more variety, don't miss cycling to Jamestown Island for a ride across the James River on the Jamestown–Scotland Ferry.

The Basics

Start: There are numerous parking areas, including the visitors centers at Yorktown, Williamsburg, and Jamestown Island. You can also park at overlooks all along the parkway.
Length: The Colonial Parkway spans 23.0 miles.
Terrain: Flat to gently rolling.
Food: Williamsburg boasts several excellent eating establishments, such as King's Arms Tavern, Raleigh Tavern, Chowning's Tavern,

and Christiana Campbell's Tavern. Yorktown and Jamestown Island have restaurants and stores as well.

For more information: American Lung Association of Virginia, Northern Region, P.O. Box 12178, Newport News, VA 23612; (800) 243–TREK. For a copy of the "Bike Map of the Historic Triangle" through Yorktown, Williamsburg, and Jamestown Island, contact: Richard C. Lockwood, State Bicycle Coordinator, Virginia Department of Highways and Transportation, 1401 E. Broad St., Richmond, VA 23219; (804) 786–2964.

Miles & Directions

You're on your own. For a National Park Service map of the entire Colonial Parkway, contact: Superintendent, Colonial National Historical Park, Yorktown, VA 23690.

43

Tidewater Cruise

Jamestown Island—Scotland
Chippokes Plantation State Park
Bacon's Castle—Surry—Scotland—Jamestown Island

Danny Bunn, of the Peninsula Bicycle Association, raves about this 30-mile ride, and with good reason. The Tidewater Cruise combines all the elements of a great bicycle tour. You'll find scenic vistas, historic intrigue, delicious regional cuisine, amusements, and excellent riding.

The ride takes off from Jamestown Island, site of the first British colony in Virginia, which dates back to the seventeenth century. Save exploration of the island for last, and head out on the route to the Jamestown–Scotland Ferry for a crossing of the James River. The ferry ride takes about twenty minutes and costs a mere 15 cents for bicyclists.

Upon landing you will pass through the fishing village of Scotland and venture out along the James River toward Chippokes Plantation State Park. Chippokes Plantation overlooks the James River. From the visitors center the route joins a bicycle trail through the park to the site of a working plantation that features an antique carriage and farm machinery. The trail follows a lane shaded by tall red cedar trees.

From Chippokes Plantation you venture onto Rte. 10 toward Bacon's Castle. A graveyard off to the right surrounds the ruins of Lower Southwark Church of the Lawns Creek Parish built in 1639, which burned in 1868. Shaded by grandfatherly oaks, the gravestones date back to the early 1800s.

Bacon's Castle is a half mile off the route on VA-617. Said to be the "oldest documented brick house in English North America," the house is famous as a stronghold established by Nathaniel Bacon, who fortified the house with rebel forces in a resistance against the tyrannical rule of Royal Governor William Berkeley.

Upon departing Bacon's Castle, the historical tour winds down in favor of a ramble through peanut, soybean, and cornfields. This second half of the ride is flat with very little traffic. If you feel the urge to put the hammer down, go ahead and work up an appetite.

The final attraction on the loop is the Surrey House, renowned for regional Virginia fare like peanut soup, the Surrey House peanut butter sandwich, peanut-raisin pie, and Virginia country-ham biscuits (Smithfield ham is processed one county over). Enjoy, it's just 4 miles back to the ferry.

On the ferry ride back to Jamestown Island, you can spot replicas of the three ships that brought the first British colonists to America: the *Godspeed, Discovery,* and *Susan Constant.* If you saved exploration of Jamestown Island for last, you'll enjoy a cool-down by cycling the 5-mile loop around the island. The National Park Service does a fine job of recreating the life-style of the early settlers.

The Basics

Start: Park at the Jamestown Settlement Visitors Center.
Length: 28.8 miles.
Terrain: Mostly flat to rolling.
Food: You'll find country stores in Scotland at 0.7 and 28.7 miles and at Bacon's Castle at 11.3. The Surrey House Restaurant and additional stores are in Surry at 24.0.
For more information: Superintendent, Colonial National Historical Park, Yorktown, VA 23690.

Miles & Directions

- 0.0 Left onto VA-31 North.
- 0.7 Enter the Jamestown–Scotland Ferry; exit ferry into Scot-

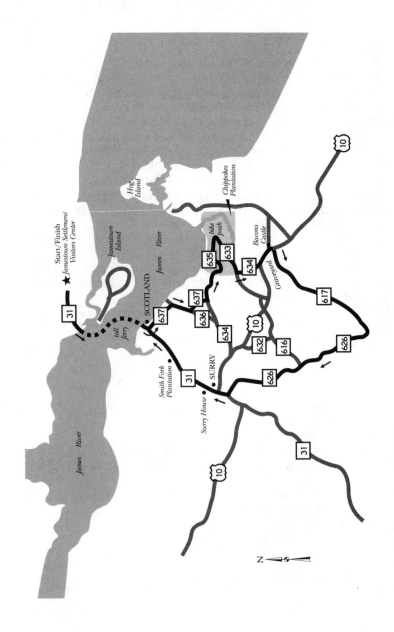

land, and follow VA-31 North.

- 0.9 In less than 0.1 mile, left onto VA-656; then left onto VA-637.
- 2.4 Right onto VA-636.
- 3.2 Left onto VA-637.
- 4.1 Left onto VA-634.
- 5.3 Left onto VA-665. Follow signs for Chippokes Plantation State Park.
- 6.1 The Chippokes Plantation State Park Visitors Center is to the left. Look for the bicycle trail to the right.
- 7.3 Right onto VA-633. (You may have to lift your bike over a gate upon exiting the park; park employees will open the gate if asked.)
- 9.1 Left onto VA-634.
- 10.2 Left onto VA-10. Look for stately graveyard on the right.
- 11.3 Right onto VA-617. Bacon's Castle is 0.5 miles from intersection on the left.
- 16.9 Right onto VA-626.
- 23.9 Right onto VA-31 South. Look for the Surrey House up ahead on the left.
- 26.2 Smith Fork Plantation on left (open for tours).
- 28.7 Approaching Scotland and the ferry entrance; exit ferry toward Jamestown Island.
- 28.8 Back at the visitors center parking lot.

44

Emporia "Great Peanut" Challenge

Skippers—Emporia—Skippers

The Emporia Bicycle Club's "Great Peanut Tour" is a party on wheels celebrating the humble peanut and the southern Virginia farm country that grows the peanut with such pride. In its thirteenth year, the "Great Peanut Tour" attracts more than 1,500 cyclists. And these cyclists know how to have a good time. Held the weekend after Labor Day, the tour features twelve bike rides ranging in length from 13 to 125 miles.

The thirteen-mile tour is a mobile social mixer where Gumby does cartwheels atop cyclists' helmets, five-year-olds pedal like mad side-by-side with the adult pack, and a black miniature poodle rides in a wicker basket on a tandem. An endless stream of cyclists stops at three farms along the route to sample peanut products and listen to talks on peanut farming and harvesting. The homemakers of Emporia surely must bake for weeks to feed peanut butter cookies, peanut butter fudge, peanut brittle, and chocolate-covered peanuts to this vast hoard of cyclists, many who admittedly bike to eat.

Nineteen ninety-one was a banner year for the Great Peanut Tour. The marriage of Brooke Pulley and David Rankin, who met on the tour in 1987, was the kickoff for the ride. Officiated by ride organizer Bobbie Wrenn, who happens to be Greenville County Clerk of Court, the couple stood up in pearl white jerseys and cycling shorts and kissed to a spray of, you guessed it, peanuts.

Bobbie Wrenn is most definitely the sparkplug behind this colorful weekend. His efforts prove that one individual can inspire involvement from an entire community. The Emporia Bicycle Club consists of a mere six members, but more than 300 volunteers ensure the event's success.

While the "Great Peanut Tour" has gained popularity through its appeal as a social event, the rides featured throughout the weekend ramble past vast farm acreage planted not only in peanuts, but also cotton and corn. At the talk on peanut farming, retired agricultural agent Bobby Flipper informed riders that Greenville County alone harvests 10,000 acres of peanut crop annually.

Featured in this ride is the Virginia *metric* century, which passes by farm after farm, wanders through the town of Emporia, and does a brief tour through the Low Ground swamp area, which separates tidewater Virginia from the piedmont. The route travels down many tree-shaded lanes.

The century route passes close by the Meherrin River. At one sag stop along the way, Peanut Tour riders marveled at the arrowhead collection of Bain Drummond. Hundreds of arrowheads and pottery fragments of the Meherrin Indians have been found within a 3-mile radius of his farm. The Meherrin Indians were a small, agrarian tribe settled along the Meherrin River in Virginia and North Carolina.

Southside Virginia is well worth the visit. Traffic on the scenic back roads is incredibly low; the residents of Greenville and Northampton counties welcome bicyclists; and the peanut and cotton fields make a pleasant backdrop for excellent touring.

In addition to the metric century, we include the thirteen-mile "Great Peanut Tour" for those looking for a quick ride.

The Basics

Start: Both rides begin at Cattail Creek R.V. Park and Campground in Skippers, Virginia (seven miles south of Emporia). Heading south on I–95, take exit 4 (old exit 1), turn left on SR-629. Go 3 miles to the campground entrance.
Miles: 13 or 62.2 miles.

Terrain: Flat with a few rolling hills.

Food: If you come for the "Great Peanut Tour" there's food everywhere. If you're exploring on your own, there are country stores throughout the metric loop. Take a side trip along Main Street around mile 30 for several restaurants in Emporia.

For more information: Emporia Bicycle Club, Inc., c/o Robert C. Wrenn, P.O. Box 631, Emporia, VA 23847; (804) 634–2222.

Miles & Directions

For the 13-mile option—

- 0.0 Begin at Cattail Creek Campground. Left onto Moore's Ferry Rd. (CR-629).
- 1.1 Left onto Massie Branch Rd. (CR-632).
- 5.7 Left onto Pine Log Rd. (CR-633).
- 6.4 Left onto Gaston Rd. (CR-603).
- 8.1 Left onto Spring Church Rd. (CR-631).
- 11.4 Left onto Moore's Ferry Rd. (CR-629).
- 13.1 End at Cattail Creek Campground.

For the 62.2-mile option—

- 0.0 Begin at the entrance to Cattail Creek Campground. Left onto Moore's Ferry Rd. (CR-629).
- 1.1 Left onto Massie Branch Rd. (CR-632)
- 5.7 Right onto Pine Log Rd. (CR-633).
- 8.5 Right onto Diamond Grove Rd. (CR-621).
- 11.8 Left onto Quarry Rd. (CR-650).
- 14.7 Left onto Rock Bridge Rd. (CR-639).
- 16.9 Left onto Brink Rd. (CR-627).
- 17.4 Right onto Independence Church Rd. (CR-633).
- 19.9 Left onto Doyle's Lake Rd. (CR-693).
- 21.4 Right onto Doyle's Lake Rd. (CR-604).
- 22.8 Right onto Dry Break Rd. (CR-611).
- 29.6 Straight on Church St.

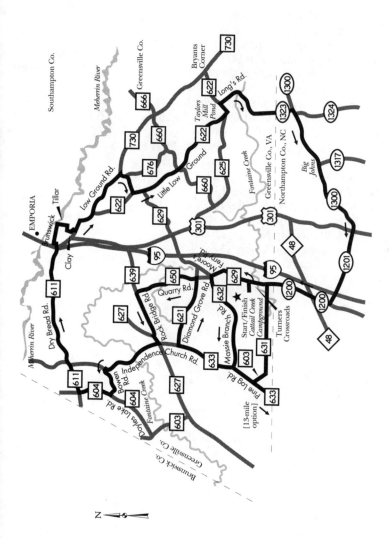

- 29.7 Left onto Everett St.
- 29.8 Right onto Brunswick Ave.
- 30.5 Straight on Hicksford Ave.
- 30.7 Right onto Tillar St.
- 31.0 Right onto Briggs St.
- 31.1 Left onto Clay St.
- 31.4 Left onto Low Ground Rd. (CR-730).
- 35.2 Right onto Brantley Moore Turnpike (CR-629).
- 35.7 Right onto Lifsey Rd. (CR-629).
- 36.5 Left onto Little Low Ground Rd. (CR-622).
- 43.0 Right onto Long's Rd. (CR-625).
- 47.0 Straight on NC Rte. 1323.
- 47.7 Right onto NC Rte. 1300.
- 50.5 Straight on NC Rte. 1300.
- 54.0 Straight on NC Rte. 1201.
- 57.5 Right onto NC Rte. 1200.
- 60.1 Straight on Moore's Ferry Rd.
- 62.2 Tour ends at Cattail Creek Campground.

Appendixes

National Cycling Organizations

League of American Wheelmen
190 West Ostend Street,
Suite 120
Baltimore, MD 21230
(301) 539–3399

United States Cycling Federation, Inc.
1750 E. Boulder St.
Colorado Springs, CO 80909
(719) 578–4581

State Cycling Organizations

The telephone numbers of many individual clubs have been omitted in compliance with club policy.

Alabama Cycling Organizations
Birmingham Bicycle Club
P.O. Box 55283
Birmingham, AL 35255
(205) 956–0897

Circle City Cycling People
c/o The Bike Shop
2417 Ross Clark Circle
Dothan, AL 36301

Spring City Cycle Club
P.O. Box 2231
Huntsville, AL 35804
(205) 533–5900

Montgomery Bicycle Club
c/o Ted Molnar
P.O. Box 17743
Montgomery, AL 36117
(205) 277–1950

Coastal Coasters Bicycle Club
10315 Blackwell Nursery Road
Semmes, AL 36575
(205) 476–6718

Florida Cycling Organizations
Boca Raton Bicycle Club
c/o Carryl Judice
1087 SW 28th Avenue
Boynton Beach, FL 33426
(407) 737–9913

Spacecoast Freewheelers
c/o Irvin Hayes
166–A N. Atlantic Avenue
Cocoa Beach, FL 32931

West Broward Freewheelers
P.O. Box 9726
Coral Springs, FL 33075

Wheelers of Kings Point
c/o Bertha Solomon
673 Saxony
Delray Beach, FL 33446

Caloosa Riders
P.O. Box 870
Fort Myers, FL 33901

South Broward Wheelers
P.O. Box 5022
Hollywood, FL 33083

Bicycle Club of Homestead
P.O. Box 0416
Homestead, FL 33034

Arlington Bicycle Club
1025 Arlington Road
Jacksonville, FL 32211

North Florida Bicycle Club
P.O. Box 14294
Jacksonville, FL 32238
(904) 387–9858

Bent's Schwinn Cyclery
c/o Steven Bent
1058 S. Florida Avenue
Lakeland, FL 33803
(813) 682–1391

Florida Bicycle Association
c/o Joanna Holt
210 Lake Hollingsworth #1707
Lakeland, FL 33803

Polk Area Bicycle Association
5100 St. Lucia Dr.
Lakeland, FL 33813

Everglades Bicycle Club
P.O. Box 430282
Miami, FL 33143

Ocala Cycling Club
P.O. Box 6036
Ocala, FL 32678

Florida Council AYH
c/o Kathy McFeely
P.O. Box 533097
Orlando, FL 32853

Florida Freewheelers Inc.
P.O. Box 547201
Orlando, FL 32854

Palm Bay Bicycle Club
c/o Jim Twigg
5275 Babcock Street, #15
Palm Bay, FL 32905

Pensacola Freewheelers Bicycling Club
c/o Dr. George Rapier, Jr.
60 Star Lake Drive
Pensacola, FL 32507
(904) 456–3528

Coastal Cruisers Bicycle Club
4613 Warm Springs Road
P.O. Box 7044
Port Charlotte, FL 33952
(813) 639–6808

St. Petersburg Bicycle Club
P.O. Box 76023
St. Petersburg, FL 33734

Sarasota Bicycle Club
P.O. Box 15053
Sarasota, FL 34277

Tampa Bay Freewheelers
c/o President
P.O. Box 8081
Tampa, FL 33674
(813) 681–3265

West Palm Beach Recreation
  B.C.
P.O. Box 6581
West Palm Beach, FL 33405

**Georgia Cycling
Organizations**

Pecan City Pedalers, Inc.
c/o William Cecile
P.O. Box 214
Albany, GA 31702

Lone Wolf Social Club of
  Columbus
c/o William D. Arnold

Columbus, GA 31909
(404) 568–1806

Emerald City Bicycle Club
c/o Charles F. Hall
507 Cardinal Drive
Dublin, GA 31021
(912) 272–0527

Chattanooga Bicycle Club
Rte. 1, Box 1319
Flintstone, GA 30725
(615) 842–4719

Gwinnett Touring Club
c/o Danny Linton
P.O. Box 597
Grayson, GA 30221
(404) 962–8153

Middle Georgia Bicycle Club
c/o Larry Gray
P.O. Box 2083
Macon, GA 31203

Southern Bicycle League
P.O. Box 1360
Roswell, GA 30077
(404) 594–8350

Coastal Bicycle Touring Club
c/o Ann Glendenning
1326 Grace Drive
Savannah, GA 31406
(912) 354–1807

Southern Cyclists
P.O. Box 2554
Statesboro, GA 30458
(912) 764–8585

Mississippi Cycling Organizations

Cycles Plus Bicycle Club
220 Main Street
Bay Saint Louis, MS 39520
(601) 467–1706

Golden Triangle Cycling Club
P.O. Box 9174
Columbus, MS 39705

Southern Cyclists
c/o J. R. Owens
201 Pecan Grove Drive
Hattiesburg, MS 39402
(601) 264–9650

Le Fleur's Bluff Bicycle Club
P.O. Box 515
Jackson, MS 39205
(601) 956–2106

Natchez Bicycle Club
c/o Claudia Soper
334 Main Street
Natchez, MS 39120
(601) 446–7794

Gulf Coast Bicycle Club
c/o Ronald Craft

2822 Belmont Drive
Ocean Springs, MS 39564

Tupelo Bicycle Club
c/o Mike Olmstead
1143 W. Main Street
Tupelo, MS 38801

North Carolina Cycling Organizations

Blue Ridge Bicycle Club
P.O. Box 309
Asheville, NC 28802

Tarheel Cyclists
P.O. Box 35392
Charlotte, NC 28235
(704) 542–2072

Carolina Tarwheels
P.O. Box 111
Durham, NC 27701
(919) 688–3458

Catawba Valley Cyclists, Inc.
P.O. Box 4241
Gastonia, NC 28053

Seyboro Cyclists
c/o Brian Brothers
P.O. Box 10741
Goldsboro, NC 27532

Triad Wheelers Bicycle Club
P.O. Box 9812

Greensboro, NC 27429
(919) 855–5540

Richmond Bike Club
c/o Mark Long
Rte. 1, Box C–46
Hamlet, NC 28345
(919) 582–6747

High Point Bicycle Club
c/o Robert Nordstrom
P.O. Box 5281
High Point, NC 27262
(919) 884–0487

Incredible Challengers
c/o Caldwell Co. Chamber of
  Commerce
223 Main Street, NW
P.O. Box 510
Lenoir, NC 28645
(704) 754–0782

Blue Ridge Outing Club
c/o Arthur DeBenigno
P.O. Box 1938
Morganton, NC 28655

North Carolina Bicycle Club
P.O. Box 32031
Raleigh, NC 27622

Piedmont Pedalers
744 Springdale
Statesville, NC 28677
(704) 873–9743

Cape Fear Cyclists
P.O. Box 3644
Wilmington, NC 28406

Piedmont Flyers Bicycle Club
P.O. Box 5032
Winston–Salem, NC 27143
(919) 768–6408

South Carolina Cycling Organizations

Aiken Bicycle Club
c/o Alan F. Riechman
P.O. Box 2073
Aiken, SC 29802
(803) 649–6950

Carolina Cyclers
P.O. Box 11163
Columbia, SC 29211

Greenville Spinners Bicycle Club
P.O. Box 2663
Greenville, SC 29602
(803) 292–6315

Spartanburg Freewheelers
P.O. Box 6171
Spartanburg, SC 29304

Tennessee Cycling Organizations

Chattanooga Bicycle Club
5360 Highway 153

Chattanooga, TN 37343
(615) 875–6811

Kennessee Cycle Club
P.O. Box 1401
Clarksville, TN 37041

Kingsport Bicycle Association
c/o Rick Heppert
P.O. Box 958
Kingsport, TN 37662
(615) 378–5302

Smoky Mountain Wheelmen
c/o Richard Fredenburg
P.O. Box 1894
Knoxville, TN 37901
(615) 637–BIKE

Memphis Hightailers Bicycle
  Club
P.O. Box 111195
Memphis, TN 38111

Bicycle Federation of Tennessee
c/o Mike Titus
P.O. Box 2823
Murfreesboro, TN 37130
(615) 893–4313

Murfreesboro Bicycle Club
c/o Mike Titus
1510 Huntington Drive, #B-5
Murfreesboro, TN 37130
(615) 893–3357

Nashville Bicycle Club
P.O. Box 158593
Nashville, TN 37215
(615) 790–3237

Highland Rimmers Bicycle Club
P.O. Box 1022
Tullahoma, TN 37388
(615) 455–8729

Virginia Cycling Organizations

Rock 'N' Road Riders, Inc.
P.O. Box 488
Blacksburg, VA 24063
(703) 951–0197

A. P. Hill/Rappahannock Bicycle
  Club
c/o James S. Day, Jr.
P.O. Box 682
Bowling Green, VA 22427
(804) 633–6500

Emporia Bicycle Club
c/o Robert C. Wrenn
P.O. Box 631
Emporia, VA 23847
(804) 634–2222

Fredericksburg Cyclists
c/o Rosemary Pitts
P.O. Box 7844
Fredericksburg, VA 22404
(703) 371–0398

Shenandoah Valley Bicycle Club
P.O. Box 1014
Harrisonburg, VA 22801

Central Virginia Bicycle Club
c/o Frank Anderson
P.O. Box 4344
Lynchburg, VA 24502
(804) 528–1914

Peninsula Bicycling Association
c/o W. H. Nuckols
P.O. Box 5639, Parkview Station
Newport News, VA 23605

Tidewater Bicycle Association
P.O. Box 12254
Norfolk, VA 23502
(804) 588–7841

Reston Bicycle Club
c/o David Heymsfeld
P.O. Box 3389
Reston, VA 22090
(703) 435–0325

Bicycle Organizations of South
 Side (BOSS)
P.O. Box 36458
Richmond, VA 23235
(804) 276–0934

Richmond Area Bicycling Club
409 N. Hamilton Street
Richmond, VA 23221

Blue Ridge Bicycle Club
c/o Artie Levin
3727 Grandin Road
Roanoke, VA 24018
(703) 774–2828

Potomac Pedalers Touring Club
P.O. Box 23601
Washington, DC 20007
(202) 363–8687

Williamsburg Bicycle Associa-
 tion
P.O. Box 713
Williamsburg, VA 23187

Winchester Wheelmen
c/o Bruce Santilli
1609 Vancouver Street
Winchester, VA 22601
(703) 667–6703

State Bicycling Maps

State bicycling maps are available free of charge. Some are available upon request at state welcome centers.

Florida Bicycle Trails
Maps and Publications Sales
Florida Dept. of Transportation
605 Suwannee Street
Tallahassee, FL 32399–0450
(904) 488–9220
 These strip maps feature seven

routes throughout Florida ranging in length from 35 to 300 miles. Facilities, state and national parks, and historic sites are covered.

Georgia Bicycle Touring Guide
Dept. of Industry, Trade and Tourism
P.O. Box 1776
Atlanta, GA 30301
(404) 656–3590
Spiral-bound strip maps covering north–south and east–west routes across the state.

Mississippi Bicycle Suitability Map
Bicycle Coordinator
Transportation Planning Division
State Highway Dept.
P.O. Box 1850
Jackson, MS 39215–1850
(601) 354–7172
This free map designates roads throughout the state as "most suitable," "suitable," and "unsuitable (high traffic volume)." State and national parks are listed; includes inset maps of recommended routes through major cities.

North Carolina Bicycling Highways
N.C. Bicycle Program
P.O. Box 25201
Raleigh, NC 27611
(919) 733–2804
The N.C. Bicycle Program has researched seven routes in the state, including the "Mountains to the Sea" route crossing the entire state. Designed as strip maps, the routes highlight facilities and historic sites.

South Carolina Bicycle Touring Guide, revised
Recreation Division
Dept. of Parks, Recreation, and Tourism
1205 Pendleton Street
Columbia, SC 29201
(803) 734–0145
A colorful, well-designed map outlining six routes throughout the state. State and national parks are highlighted. Addresses for additional information are listed.

Tennessee Bicycling Highways
Dept. of Tourist Development
Att'n: Bike Maps
P.O. Box 23170
Nashville, TN 37202
(615) 741–2158

These maps outline four touring routes in Tennessee, highlighting state parks, services, and points of interest.

Southeast Region

Bikecentennial
P.O. Box 8308
Missoula, MT 59807
(406) 721–1776

Bikecentennial has developed a network of bicycle-touring route maps throughout the United States. The southeastern states are prominent in two of their routes: The "Virginia to Florida Bicycle Route" travels from Richmond, Virginia, to Ft. Myers Beach, Florida. The famous "Transamerican Bicycle Trail" crosses Virginia from Christianburg to Yorktown.

Bicycle Touring Companies

Asheville Bicycle Adventures
Rte. 1, Box 147 Brevard Road
Arden, NC 28704
(704) 687–3636

Mountain-bike tours in the Blue Ridge Mountains. Full and half-day tours.

Backroads Bicycle Touring
1516 5th Street, Suite 6D
Berkeley, CA 94710-1740
1 (800) 245–3874

Backroads Bicycle Touring leads tours through the North Carolina Outer Banks and the Shenandoah Valley in Virginia.

Carolina Bike Tours
2015 Wolcott Avenue
Wilmington, NC 28403
(919) 762–3931 or (919) 762–5007

Carolina Bike Tours offers tours from Wilmington along the Cape Fear River for an overnight stay at Bald Head Island.

Carolina Cycle Tours
41 US Hwy. 19 West
Bryson City, NC 28713
(704) 488–6737

A division of the Nantahala Outdoor Center, Carolina Cycle Tours offers road- and mountain-bike tours of the Southeast, which cover Florida, the Blue Ridge Mountains, and the Natchez Trace Parkway.

Classic Bicycle Tours and Treks
P.O Box 668
Clarkson, NY 14430
(800) 777–8090

Classic Bicycle Tours features tours along the Natchez Trace Parkway in Tennessee and Mississippi.

Suwannee Bicycle Association, Inc.
P.O. Box 247
White Springs, FL 32096
Led by Lys Burden and affiliated with the Florida Council of American Youth Hostels, Suwannee Bicycle Association, Inc. features a monthly "Suwannee Century Series," which follows a variety of 100-mile routes from White Springs. The association is also the sponsor of the "Spirit of the Suwannee ATB Get–away Weekend" in October.

Vermont Country Cyclers
P.O. Box 145
Dept. 232
Waterbury Center, VT 05677-0145
(802) 244–5135
Vermont Country Cyclers offers tours in Virginia, North Carolina, and central Florida.

About the Authors

Because of their sustained interest in bicycling, both as a sport and a form of recreation, Elizabeth and Charles Skinner have written this, their second book on the subject. Their first is *Bicycling the Blue Ridge: A Guide to the Skyline Drive and the Blue Ridge Parkway*. Their affiliation with the League of American Wheelmen and several regional organizations further exemplifies their dedication to bicycling.

Elizabeth Skinner is currently a branch manager in the Winston-Salem/Forsyth County Public Library System, while Charles, her husband, is employed at Gravely International, a tractor manufacturer. The Skinners reside in Pfafftown, a suburb of Winston-Salem, North Carolina.

Best Bike Rides
Short Bike Rides
Short Nature Walks

Here are the other fine titles offered in the **Best Bike Rides**, **Short Bike Rides**, and **Short Nature Walks** series, created for those who enjoy recreational cycling and nature walks. Please check your local bookstore for other Globe Pequot Press outdoor recreation titles.

The Best Bike Rides in New England, $12.95
The Best Bike Rides in the Pacific Northwest, $12.95
Short Bikes Rides Greater Boston Central MA, $16.95
Short Bikes Rides in and around Washington, D.C., $8.95
Short Bikes Rides Eastern Pennsylvania, $8.95
Short Bikes Rides in Rhode Island, $8.95
Short Bikes Rides Cape Cod, Nantucket, Vineyard, $8.95
Short Bikes Rides in Connecticut, $8.95
Short Bikes Rides in Long Island, $8.95
Short Bikes Rides in New Jersey, $8.95
Short Bikes Rides in and around New York City, $8.95
Short Nature Walks on Long Island, $8.95
Short Nature Walks Cape Cod and the Vineyard, $8.95
Sixty Selected Short Nature Walks in Connecticut, $8.95

To order any of these titles with MASTERCARD or VISA, call toll-free 1-800-243-0495; in Connecticut call 1-800-962-0973. Free shipping for orders of three or more books. Shipping charge of $3.00 per book for one or two books ordered. Connecticut residents add sales tax. Ask for free catalogue of Globe Pequot's quality books on recreation, travel, nature, gardening, cooking, crafts, and more. Prices subject to change.